# CLINICAL PSYCHOLOGY:

## A Social Psychological Approach

**Peter L. Sheras**
**Stephen Worchel**
*University of Virginia*

VNR VAN NOSTRAND REINHOLD COMPANY
NEW YORK    CINCINNATI    ATLANTA    DALLAS    SAN FRANCISCO
LONDON        TORONTO        MELBORNE

Van Nostrand Reinhold Company Regional Offices:
New York    Cincinnati    Atlanta    Dallas    San Francisco

Van Nostrand Reinhold Company International Offices:
London    Toronto    Melbourne

Library of Congress Catalog Card Number: 79-4473
ISBN: 0-442-25208-0

Manufactured in the United States of America

Published by Van Nostrand Reinhold Company
135 West 50th Street, New York, N.Y. 10020

Published simultaneously in Canada by Van Nostrand Reinhold Ltd.

15 14 13 12 11 10 9 8 7 6 5 4 3 2 1          $616 \cdot 89$
                                             $\not{A} 551$

**Library of Congress Cataloging in Publication Data**

Sheras, Peter L
    Clinical psychology.

    Bibliography: p.
    Includes index.
    1. Clinical psychology.    2. Social psychology.
I.    Worchel, Stephen, joint author.    II. Title.
[DNLM: 1. Psychology, Clinical.    2. Psychology,
Social. WM105 S551c]
RC467.S482          616.8'9          79-4473
ISBN 0-442-25208-0

To our wives
Phyllis Koch-Sheras and Frances Worchel.

# Preface

An increasingly common pastime of psychologists is to bemoan the "crisis" in the field. Social psychologists lament the fact that the 1970's have been a period of few new theories of social behavior or new methodologies for the study of this behavior. Experimental psychologists have increasingly observed that there seems to be less interest in basic research. Clinical psychologists, too, have begun to question the lack of unifying theory between clinical behavior and the rapid but often unrelated proliferation of "clinical techniques."

While the 1970's may be seen by some as the "age of crisis" in psychology, the decade may more accurately be characterized as the "age of self-reflection." Over the past fifty years, the field of psychology has grown at a tremendous rate, resulting in increasing specialization and fragmentation. Fifty years ago, if someone said he or she was a psychologist, it would be safe to assume that the person was engaged in experimentation on learning, perception, or the physiological basis of behavior. Today, we must ask a number of questions in order to determine "what that person actually does." Is he or she an experimental psychologist, a physiological psychologist, a developmental psychologist, a social psychologist, a clinical psychologist, an educational psychologist, a community psychologist, or a parapsychologist? Is he or she engaged in the delivery of psychological services, the teaching of psychology, or in experimentation? Does he or she work with animals, children, or adults? Is the orientation behavioristic, humanistic, or cognitive?

The questions are necessary to determine not only

what a particular psychologist does but also what psychological language that person speaks and what body of psychological literature he or she is likely to be familiar with. The increasing fragmentation in psychology has created many specialists, and the generalist or the renaissance psychologist has all but disappeared. Further, the specialists have often "gone their own way," and communication between the specialists has become more and more difficult and less and less common.

Increasing specialization has had both positive and negative consequences. On the positive side, the specialization has yielded in-depth understanding of various aspects of human behavior. Theories and techniques have been refined to give concise answers to questions in very specific areas. A voluminous body of knowledge has been developed in each of the subareas of psychology.

While this specialization has facilitated the understanding of specific aspects of human behavior, a negative consequence has been that a broad understanding of the dynamics of the individual seems farther away than ever. It is as if we had achieved some knowledge about how the individual "parts" of the human being function but now found ourselves preplexed about the question of how these parts fit and function together.

This is the picture that has emerged as psychologists have entered this "age of self-reflection." It is a disquieting picture for a scholar truly interested in the phenomenon of total human behavior, and the recent years have been marked by attempts to alter this trend in psychology. More and more, psychologists have attempted to overcome the psychological straightjacket of specialization. Communication is becoming increasingly common between psychologists in various subareas. Clinical psychologists, social psychologists, and environmental psychologists have worked together to study the problems of the community. Experimental psychologists, developmental psychologists, and educational psychologists have combined expertise to examine the efficacy of various classroom teaching methods. Psychologists from the various subareas have worked together in studying such questions as integration, the problems of the elderly, and effects of environment on behavior.

Our belief that this "coming together" of psychologists from the various subfields is healthy both for psychology and for society in general motivated us to write this book. We each have had training in the areas of social and clinical psychology and felt that a closer relationship of the two areas would benefit both. Social psychology is a field characterized by a healthy preoccupation with developing theory and research methods to study human behavior. It has also been criticized as a field that is anemic when it comes to applying the lessons learned from the theories and research. Clinical psychology, on the other hand, is a field where application rules and theory and research are often relegated to the role of second-class citizens. Both areas are concerned with the dynamics of interpersonal behavior, and hence, a marriage of the two areas would seem "a natural."

In reality, this volume should be viewed as a proposal for marriage rather than the marriage itself. Our aim is to show that a closer union between social and clinical psychology would be enriching to both. We have attempted to explore one of the areas where such a union could be made by concentrating on the therapy session itself. The therapy session is an integral part of applied clinical psychology. The particular technique is often chosen because the therapist has a "feeling" that "it will work." In most cases there is little research showing whether the technique actually does work or why it works. The therapy session provides a clear example of where social psychology might be used to supply the answer to the question of "why." The session involves interpersonal interaction; this is true whether the therapy is individual, couple, family, or group. Theories and research in social psychology are aimed specifically at explicating interpersonal interaction. They have been concerned with determining why people are attracted to

viii      Preface

each other, why they aggress against one another, why they conform or deviate, why people hold particular attitudes and how these attitudes affect their behavior, how people communicate their feelings, and the dynamics involved when people work in groups.

The aim of this volume is to show that these theories can be applied to explain why therapy sessions proceed as they do and what variables are likely to determine the direction of this progress, rather than to give an exhaustive demonstration of *how* they can be applied. The latter task is well beyond the scope of this book. We do hope that in showing the feasibility of the application, we will stimulate the reader to investigate further how the application can be made. For ourselves, as scientists and practitioners, we have begun the process of combination and crossvalidation of these two subareas, and this volume is a product of the enthusiasm generated in us by our own attempts.

While the responsibility for this volume must rest on the shoulders of the authors, many others were instrumental in its publication. First we would like to thank our wives, Phyllis Koch-Sheras and Frances Worchel, who not only made insightful comments on the manuscript but also provided the moral support that bolstered our sometimes flagging spirits and allowed us to complete the project. M. Alan Jacobowitz of Trenton State College, Richard M. Ryckman of the University of Maine at Orono, and Robert L. Woolfolk of Rutgers University, along with Philip Worchel and Jason Worchel, made penetrating and helpful comments on some or all of the chapters. The labors of Peggy Marshall, Diane Nataline, Debra Mundie, Hazel Shifflett, and Louise Spangler, who often put everything else aside to type a chapter that was "due last week" are gratefully acknowledged. Finally, we would like to thank Judith Joseph and Jeanne Libby for their tireless effort in guiding this project through the many valleys of authors' peril to a successful completion.

Peter Sheras
Stephen Worchel

# Contents

# Chapter 1

# Introduction

An increasingly common complaint echoed by many people is that the world has become so complicated and segmented that they have little time to get acquainted with their neighbors. Individuals who have lived next door to each other for years are almost total strangers. They may know only their neighbor's name or have a superficial passing acquaintance, but the relationship extends no farther. A similar situation exists within the field of psychology. In the last century a number of subfields of psychology have developed. Though having common roots and often being interested in similar problems these subfields have largely "gone their own way." It is a rarity today to hear of someone being referred to as a "psychologist;" instead we have "clinical psychologists," "developmental psychologists," "social psychologists," "experimental psychologists," "physiological psychologists." The list could go on and on.

Much like the neighbors who are strangers, so too the psychologists in the different subareas have become strangers. Each subfield has developed its own "language" and staked out its own territory for study. The increasing estrangement of the different subareas of psychology may be partly the inevitable consequence of the complexity of these subareas. Psychologists often lament, "I wish I knew more about the other areas but I just don't have the time if I'm really going to learn my own area."

While this fragmentation of psychology may have the

1

beneficial effect of allowing the development of a high degree of expertise, the cost to the discipline as a whole is extremely high. This is especially the case when two subareas study very similar problems but fail to learn from each other. When this happens both subareas lose an important opportunity for cross-fertilization and an enrichment of their understanding of a common problem.

While there are many places in psychology where a reacquaintance of "wayward siblings" would be tremendously profitable to both, one of the clearest examples exists in social psychology and clinical psychology. Social psychology involves "the study of the way in which individuals are affected by social situations" (Worchel and Cooper, 1976, p. 7). As we will see in the next section, social psychologists have focused their attention on developing precise theories to explain why individuals are influenced in a specific manner. They have also developed rigorous experimental methods for testing these theories. As a result of wedding the theories and experimentation, social psychology has amassed a tremendous body of experimentally substantiated knowledge about the effect of social situations on the individual. The field has, however, been criticized for its reluctance to apply its knowledge to explaining or solving social problems. In essence, it is a field with great academic credentials but little practical experience.

Clinical psychology, on the other hand, has been the object of a different criticism. Like social psychology, much of the concerns of the clinician involve the effects of social situations on individuals. The individual's social environment is often viewed as a major contributing factor in emotional disturbances. The identification and especially the treatment of these disturbances involve social interaction. As we will see later in this book, this is true whether the treatment employs individual or group therapy techniques. Traditionally, the clinician has focused attention on developing social environments that offer effective treatment for the specific problem at hand. This practical orientation has given rise to a wide variety of treatment programs such as psychoanalysis, client-centered therapy, Gestalt therapy, encounter groups, and behavioral therapy to name a few. Thus clinical psychology has become largely an application-oriented field whose aim has been to manipulate the social situation to achieve the greatest therapeutic advantages. Questions have been raised about why a certain therapy is successful, what are the social dynamics of therapy, and what is the proof that the therapy is, indeed, successful. Essentially these criticisms point toward the lack of experimentation and theory associated with many of the treatment aspects of clinical psychology. Techniques often spring up because they "seem to work" but questions about why they work are often left unanswered or only partially answered.

Thus, we have two subareas of psychology that are concerned, at least in large part, with a common problem: the effect of the social situation on the individual. One area's strength is the other area's weakness. This commonality of interest and complementarity of strength should serve as an ideal combination for exchange of knowledge and joint investigation by clinical and social psychologists. Unfortunately, this has not been the case. Until recently, with a few exceptions, each area has been content to focus on its own self-development.

The aim of this volume is to offer suggestions about how the chasm between the two areas can be bridged. Our interest is to demonstrate where commonalities between the two fields exist and how the strengths of the two areas can be utilized in examining problems of mutual interest. We will attempt to point out where possibilities for future dialogue exist between the two fields. It would be premature to attempt to do more since there is so little joint research at this time

The focus of this book will be on the dynamics involved in psychotherapy rather than on the etiology of emotional disturbances. We chose this focus because the therapy setting so clearly involves a social setting and there has been little empirical research on the dynamics involved in that setting. Before discussing the social dynamics of psychotherapy, it will be helpful to quickly outline the histories of social and clinical psychology. This review should serve to place the discussion of therapy into a clearer context.

## A BRIEF HISTORY OF
## SOCIAL PSYCHOLOGY

The history of social psychology is relatively easy to trace since it is a very young science. While William McDougall published a social psychology text in 1908, most social psychologists trace their lineage back only to the middle 1930s. The early works in social psychology attempted to explain human behavior by positing the existence of a number of natural instincts. For example, McDougall suggested that human beings act aggressively because they have an instinct to behave violently. This instinct approach has a number of limitations, the most serious being that it cannot adequately explain the richness and variety in human behavior. We all know some people who often act aggressively and others who seldom aggress. Some of our friends are likely to use verbal aggression while others may physically "strike out" when angry. An instinct theory of aggression could not explain this wide range of aggressive behaviors.

In the late 1930s, Kurt Lewin offered a new approach to social psychology that served as the foundation for the field as it exists today (Lewin, 1935; 1938). In addition to conducting a number of important experiments, Lewin taught two important lessons that guided the field. The first was that "nothing is so practical as a good theory." While Lewin was concerned with helping to solve a number of pressing social problems of his day, he felt that attempts to solve these problems would be of limited value if theories about social behavior were not simultaneously developed. A good theory would allow the researcher to become un-chained from a specific event and apply his findings to a much broader range of problems. Thus, Lewin strenuously pushed social psychologists to develop theories.

The second position in which Lewin strongly believed was the necessity of conducting rigorous experimentation to test the validity of the theories. Lewin himself conducted numerous experiments in the areas of leadership and group dynamics. He was one of the founders of the T-group movement. However, his interest in the T-group was not so much in its therapeutic qualities but in the opportunities it offered for experimentation in group dynamics.

Lewin's students endorsed these two positions and the field of social psychology turned its attention to theory development and experimental methodology. Less atten-tion was given to supplying temporary solutions to the social problems of the period, although much of the re-search and theory was motivated by these problems. For example, during World War II one of the pressing problems was to get the American housewife to change her cooking habits. A shortage of the most popular beef cuts was developing in the United States. There was, however, an abundance of beef entrails such as liver, sweetbreads, and brains. The problem was to convince the American housewife to serve these entrails to her family. Lewin (1943) conducted a study aimed at identifying the most efficient means to create this behavior change. While his study was linked to a pressing social problem, it is important to note that Lewin conducted a careful experiment and used the results of the study to further develop his force field theory of human behavior.

A similar problem arose during the late 1950s and early 1960s. The United States was involved in a Cold War and an arms race with the Russians. Social psychologists such as Morton Deutsch and Robert Krauss (1960) conducted a number of laboratory studies on bargaining and bargaining strategies. As with Lewin, the impetus for the research grew out of a social problem but the researchers worked to develop a careful methodology and theory that could be applied beyond the question of tactics in the Cold War.

The 1950s and early 1960s saw intense efforts to develop social psychological theories. The theories of cognitive dissonance, social comparison, attribution, and social learning were published, along with theories of conformity, attitude change, group dynamics, interpersonal attraction, and conflict. While the theories themselves were often inspired by current social problems, they were not limited to these specific problems. As a result, some criticism was aimed at social psychology for not showing enough concern about the problems existing in society.

With the development of a large number of theories came vigorous efforts to test the validity of the theories and to refine them. The 1960s and 1970s were characterized by a tremendous explosion in the number of experiments in social psychology. New methodologies were devised and great effort was given to testing each detail of the theories. A large majority of the research was conducted in laboratory settings because only in this setting could the necessary experimental control be achieved. This was a critical period in the life of social psychology because any science is only as good as its theories and methodologies. One result of this concern for methodology was that social psychology gained increased respect in the scientific community. Another result was an increase in the criticism of the field for seemingly showing a lack of sensitivity to events outside the social psychological laboratory.

Armed with an arsenal of theories and methodologies, social psychologists have began turning their attention to this criticism. In the 1970s social psychologists have shown increasing interest in applying their knowledge to events outside the laboratory. Experiments and applications are currently found in such areas as education, women's studies, environmental influences on behavior, advertising, law, race relations, and urban studies. This trend is likely to continue as the social psychological theories are readily applicable to these areas. They are also very relevant to many of the areas of clinical psychology, as we will show later in this book.

## A BRIEF HISTORY OF CLINICAL PSYCHOLOGY

At the outset, the history of clinical psychology should be differentiated from that of psychiatry. Although most recently clinical psychology as a discipline has been associated with the field of psychiatry, its roots are clearly in psychology and its history. Psychiatry, pioneered in the late nineteenth century by the seminal works of Kraepelin and others, was clearly a subfield of medicine and as such was concerned with the diagnosis and treatment of disease. Even the major contributions of Sigmund Freud between 1899 and 1939, which are often considered to be central to the psychological study of personality, were the works of Freud the physician and neurologist.

Clinical psychology as a subfield of psychology had its roots in the late 1800s with the work of a number of scientists whose major concern was not the treatment of disease per se, but understanding and assessing the sensory and psychological functions.

Lightner Witmer, a student of Wilhelm Wundt, is considered by some to be the originator of clinical psychology. In 1896, he founded the first psychological clinic in America at the University of Pennsylvania. The focus of this clinic and the early work of clinical psychologists was the treatment of speech disorders, sensory dysfunctions, and learning problems. Most of the clients, and those that followed over the next two decades, were children. Indeed, the major contribution made to the area of clinical psychology during the next twenty years was in the area of child guidance. The child guidance movement, however, focused mostly upon the behavioral problems of the children treated. Many of these problems were social in nature, such as juvenile delinquency and severe acting out in younger children. It is clear in retrospect, however, that a number of children now thought to be psychotic were treated in these guidance centers. Many of these child guidance centers are still in existence.

A parallel and, perhaps, more important trend in the development of clinical psychology can be seen in the work of the French psychologist Binet and his followers, who concentrated on the creation of the first tests of intelligence. Their development of the Stanford-Binet scale and its extensive use marked the first wide acceptance of clinical psychology. It is important to note that these tests of intelligence were the first real applied methods available to clinicians which could yield measurable results.

Two other movements in clinical psychology are worth mentioning in the period prior to 1940. They are the mental hygiene movement and the emergence of the study of abnormal psychology.

In the first part of the twentieth century, some psychologists became interested in the care and treatment of hospitalized mental "defectives," or those who were considered to have disorders of the personality. Attempts at treatment soon demonstrated the complexity of the problems involved and there emerged an interest in understanding the etiology of the disorders. The realization of the need to understand more fully the cause of these "mental disorders" led to the growing acceptance of abnormal psychology as a legitimate field of study.

Thus, the early history of clinical psychology proceeded along a number of lines both theoretical and applied, although it seems clear that the applied aspects of the child guidance, testing, and mental hygiene movements received the most attention. The advent of the Second World War, however, had by far the greatest influence on the development of modern clinical psychology.

World War II brought to light the need for a better understanding of the connection between psychological disturbances and behavior. Two major realizations contributed to the determination of this need. The first was the high incidence of psychological deferments awarded to draftees. It became obvious that psychological problems were much wider spread throughout the population than had been previously believed. The second important discovery was the number of combat-related psychological problems which began to appear. It was, therefore, the military which saw the greatest need for the treatment of psychological difficulties, and it was primarily through its support that clinical psychology began to establish itself as a legitimate field of study and treatment.

Most of the work performed by psychologists in the military was of an applied nature, attempting to treat the effects of battle-related psychological problems. In addition, clinical psychologists began to develop instruments for assessing personality and the psychological factors which might affect a person's susceptibility to emotional or psychological troubles. This work was done with application in mind.

Following the war, a number of conferences took place to define the field of clinical psychology and to set up the mechanisms for the training of clinical psychologists. This education was seen as an experiment to train professionals in the "scientist-practitioner" model. According to this conception of training and practice, the clinical psychologist was to be a scientist by training as well as practitioner by vocation. In the years to follow, however, the profession of clinical psychology has emphasized the applied aspect both in training and in practice. In the past five years, especially, there has been a marked increase in the professional training of clinicians weighted heavily toward assessment and therapy and less and less toward theory for its own sake. There has developed a schism even within the discipline which has produced two schools of clinical training, one emphasizing research and the other clinical practice. Even in research, the emphasis has always been more on application in clinical settings than on the construction of theory.

More recently, however, clinicians have begun to realize that the theoretical insights of other related disciplines may be of use to them in their clinical training and practice. Clinicians have begun to see the use of theory to help them understand the complexities of the therapy situation. More and more, "models" of therapy are being explored. These models can draw heavily on the existing theory of human interaction in social psychology.

## THE ORIENTATION AND FORMAT OF THIS BOOK

In this volume we will describe how some of the theoretical constructs in social psychology may apply to current psychotherapies in use by clinical psychologists. No attempt will be made to pass judgment upon the usefulness or effectiveness of these therapies or orientations. We merely would like to demonstrate that these treatment modalities may knowingly or unknowingly embrace the principles of social psychology. The therapies discussed are examples of some of those in current practice. The list is not meant to be exhaustive. We make the assumption that all psychotherapy employs some social psychological concepts and that some of the success of therapy may be due to reasons explainable by social psychologists as well as clinical psychologists. We wish to demonstrate that therapy techniques and skills may be seen in the "context" of social psychological theories. We do not advocate the social psychological perspective as being any better than the clinical one, merely different and, therefore, hopefully of some use in understanding why people change in psychotherapy.

For the most part, this book will adopt the social psychological perspective toward understanding the process of psychotherapy. We will not attempt to examine the efficacy of therapy modalities, styles, or schools of thought, or even of therapy in general. Different styles and approaches will be discussed to demonstrate how some social psychological forces may be enhanced in the performance of certain therapies, however.

This is not a manual on how to do therapy. All of the cases mentioned and the therapies discussed are meant to serve as examples, not as prototypes of the therapy process. We will, however, attempt to integrate some of the information provided by social psychological theory with actual clinical situations and methods. We hope the demonstration of the vast overlap in the subject matter of social and clinical psychology will be used to the benefit of both groups. This overlap, we believe, will be shown not only in the obvious areas of groups and group dynamics, but also the general area of interpersonal relationship, a prerequisite for effective clinical work.

It is important for us to be clear that we do not think that clinical psychology is just social psychology, or that a knowledge of social psychological theory will by itself make for effective and competent clinicians. Rather, we are trying to explore the contribution that an understanding of social psychology can make to the understanding of clinical psychology treatment issues and practices. With these understandings we believe that the effectiveness of therapy may be increased in some cases and a better understanding of why therapy of a certain type or style is already so successful can emerge.

The format of this book is designed to acquaint the reader with some of the basic concepts in both the social and clinical psychological disciplines, as well as to develop an idea of how and when these concepts come into play in the execution of therapy. The four major chapters to follow will explore the four major modalities of therapy in use today: individual psychotherapy, group therapy, couples counseling, and family therapy. Each chapter begins with the brief presentation of a case. The case material is designed to give a flavor of what the most frequent events in this sort of therapy might look like. It is not presented in scrupulous detail as it is not meant to be a prototype of therapy, merely an example. The case is referred to throughout the remainder of each chapter to make clear the dynamics being explained. Each case is presented to demonstrate something about the "process" of therapy, not average "content." The cases have been selected because of the dynamics they portray, not the concrete issues talked about in the sessions. It is not as important to see what couples argue about, for instance, as it is to see *how* it is that they argue.

Following the case study, each chapter will present the major theories in social psychology which bear on the process of the case and on that particular modality of therapy (e.g., individual, group, etc.). Along with the theories, research is presented to clarify the concepts involved. As we have seen, there is unfortunately, at this point in time, very little research in the relationship of social and clinical psychology. We present, therefore, the relevant social psychological research and attempt to relate it to the clinical setting. The theories presented in this second part of each chapter are, in many cases, merely a sampling of some of the relevant ideas. They are not meant to be exhaustive or complete as the scope of this book cannot provide more than a limited amount of space.

The third section in each chapter presents and discusses the application of social psychological theory in the clinical situation. In some instances specific schools of thoughts are presented (e.g., Gestalt therapy) and in others where schools of thought are not as important in clinical practice, general discussion of the effects of social psychology phenomena is presented. This section attempts to examine how an understanding of the concepts in the second section is used in the treatment setting. Again, all of the connections cannot be made, but important examples are given. Selected readings are provided for those who wish to explore more of the connections.

## CONCLUSION

The purpose of this volume is not to assert that social and clinical psychology are the same. Rather, we are attempting to explore a new, integrated perspective which calls upon the theoretical strengths of social psychology and the applied knowledge which exists in clinical psychology. Our hope is that this book will foster new cooperation between two subdisciplines within psychology, a cooperation we believe to have incredible potential for the advancement of the understanding of human interaction and treatment.

## SELECTED READINGS

Corsini, Raymond (ed.). *Current Psychotherapies*. Itasca, Ill.: F. E. Peacock Publishers, 1973.

Garfield, Sol. *Clinical Psychology: The Study of Personality and Behavior*. Chicago: Aldine, 1974.

Worchel, S., and Cooper, J. *Understanding Social Psychology*. Homewood, Ill.: Dorsey Press, 1979.

Chapter 2

# Individual Therapy

## CASE STUDY

John sat looking blankly at the advertisement in the *New Yorker*, his favorite magazine. He caught himself staring and brought his mind back into the small room he was sitting in. It was the waiting room of a psychologist's office. It looked pretty much like any waiting room. John looked around the room for a hint of what it might be like in the inner office. "I hope Dr. Williams and I have something in common," he thought. John liked the photographs in the waiting room and began to wonder if Dr. Williams had taken them. John was an avid photographer himself when he was not working at his job as a reader at a local publishing house. "I hope I like this guy," he thought almost out loud.

John's mind was still a bit foggy. He began to reflect on how he came to be sitting here now. Usually at this time he was playing softball with his friends from the office. He imagined what they were doing now and hoped this appointment would be worthwhile. He really loved to play and was giving it up to be here now. He was a little angry about that, but he thought that what he was doing here now might be more important. His mind began to wander again. He remembered the first "incident" in his mind, now six weeks in the past. Standing at the checkout counter at the supermarket he had suddenly been overcome by panic. He began to shake uncontrollably and dropped a half-gallon bottle of orange juice which shattered on the floor. John had been taken completely by surprise. He had never had such a feeling in his twenty-five years and was worried and confused. The panic seemed so sudden and severe that he didn't know what to think. It was like being hit over the head with a baseball bat. Later that day he had told his girlfriend of the event. She was also confused and a bit concerned. She suggested that if it was worrying him he might get some help with the problem from a therapist. John was very unsure about going into psychotherapy. He knew it would take time and probably a lot of money. Was the incident that strange and scary?

A week later, however, while at the hardware store buying some picture hooks, he again had the same feeling. He began to shake all over and had to run outside onto the sidewalk before the feeling would subside. In his haste he ran out of the store with the hooks still in his hand without paying for them. Now John was even more concerned. He decided not to tell Betty, his girlfriend, about this event as he thought she might get more worried, or might even think he was crazy. John got on the bus and tried to think of something else. As soon as he sat down, though, he began to have that same quivering in the pit of his stomach. He began to sweat profusely. He was sure that everyone on the bus must be looking at him and thinking he was weird. He got off the bus at the next stop and walked home. By the time he reached his front door he decided that he needed to do something about what was happening to him. He was very unsure about asking for some help from anyone. It seemed so weak and unstable. Then he decided that he might just see what a psychologist had to say. John could always leave if he wanted to, he thought. He called Betty and got the name of a psychologist that had helped one of her friends.

Despite his resolve, John put off making an appointment for a week. During that time he avoided any small places filled with people. When he finally did call, the only time Dr. Williams could see him was during his softball game. That almost changed his mind, but he decided that it might be worth missing just one game. He would need to see about missing others, though. But the appointment was made now and a short week later (or so it seemed) he was sitting in the office waiting for the therapist to appear.

John began to experience that quivering in his stomach. For a moment he thought he might have another "attack," but he managed to control his fear by picking up another magazine and leafing through the pages. He tried to think about the meeting that was ahead of him. What would it be like? Was Dr. Williams as good as Betty had said? What was going to happen to him in that office? Would he be made to cry, reveal some sensitive part of his past, talk about his sexual relationships or childhood? All these questions raced through his mind and made his stomach sink. Just then the inner office door opened and a tall man in his early thirties appeared.

"John?" the voice said softly. "Please come in."

John looked carefully at the figure in the doorway. A thousand thoughts raced through his head. The doctor was much younger than John expected: no beard or glasses. He looked a lot like some of the people John knew at work. He was a little surprised and hesitant. In an instant John found himself walking almost automatically into the inner office. He glanced around the new room looking for a couch and dark mysterious atmosphere, but saw only a desk and a few stuffed chairs.

"Sit down, John." Dr. Williams pointed to one of the chairs. "My name is Frank. Why don't you tell me a little about what brought you to see me?"

He looked at Frank carefully. Frank seemed sympathetic and friendly, but John's words stuck in his throat as he tried to respond.

"I know this may be a bit difficult for you in the beginning," Frank said, "but we have plenty of time to get to know each other. Many people feel a bit nervous in the beginning. It's natural to think you are afraid."

During the next hour John basically talked with Frank. Nothing mysterious happened. Frank asked John to describe the attacks and his feelings about what had happened, why John thought it had happened, and some questions about his life, past and present. John had been completely mystified about the origin of his problem. Frank asked him to describe his feelings about the attacks. Did he think he was losing his mind? Frank asked him to imagine the scene in the supermarket with his eyes closed and to describe the feelings he was having at that moment in the session and to "experience" them as fully as he could. At first John became frightened and felt the quivering in his stomach but he found that as he described the physical sensations he was having to Frank, the panic he was feeling began to dissipate. He was surprised that he could begin to experience those sensations that had been so frightening to him before and get to the end of them without an "attack." Frank asked John to describe how he was feeling about being in therapy and in general explored his feelings and fears about other things that were happening in his life now: his job, his relationship with Betty, his feelings for his parents. The more he spoke, the more comfortable John felt. He was able to look Frank in the eye and could speak without feeling nervous or feeling that Frank was judging or evaluating him. At the end of the hour John felt better about the therapy although he was still not sure about whether it would actually keep him from having another "attack."

Frank and John discussed continuing therapy. John made a commitment to pay for the sessions. The fee was high but John was hoping that would make him work hard on getting to the bottom of his problem. He was surprised that Frank made the decisions of when to meet and how often with him, not for him. Still, John felt he could choose to stop therapy at any time.

Over time John began to trust his therapist and share more about what he was feeling about himself. He was not always sure how to make sense of what was happening, but Frank helped him to clarify his feelings and thoughts. After a few months, John felt better about himself. He knew he was not crazy. He began to think that something had triggered his attacks and he had to find out what it was. Frank taught him how to relax and say some things to himself when he thought he might have an attack. John also began to fear the attacks less and began to feel a bit more in control of what was happening.

Slowly, John felt better and more in control of himself. He looked forward to the therapy sessions as an energizing part of his week. He also talked more and more about his fears as an adolescent, especially fears about his father. John's father was a large, strong man with a booming voice and he commanded the household (John's mother and two older brothers). John remembered being quizzed at the dinner table about his activities in school and sent to his room with a harsh word and a wave of his father's hand if he did not live up to his father's expectation. John tried hard to please his father but never felt as successful as either of his brothers. He resented his father but was always too frightened to say so. He wanted his father to love him but never felt that he did. He wanted his father to know that he was loved by his youngest son, but never had a chance to tell him that. John went to college, moved away from home, and had only a casual relationship with his parents. John wanted to tell his father what he felt about him, but before he graduated from college, his father died unexpectedly.

In one session, while talking about the fear he felt in talking to his father, John remembered that when he was eleven or so his father had slapped him in public and berated him for wanting to buy a cigarette lighter. He remembered there being a lot of people around and he felt incredibly angry at his father and ashamed. When he remembered this, John knew it was important because he began to have that feeling in his stomach. Frank explored the issues of the relationship John had with his father and supported him for the feelings he had of fear, hate, and love. Frank made it clear that those feelings were appropriate at that time and that the therapy now would help him get in touch with the feelings and work them out. Frank made John feel that his case was not at all hopeless, but would just take some time to work with.

Over a period of months, John began to fear having an attack less and less. He was more open about what he felt and his attacks made more sense to him. Frank worked with him using a number of techniques to explore strategies for expressing and dealing with his fear.

## SOCIAL DYNAMICS OF INDIVIDUAL THERAPY

### Setting the Stage

Oftentimes efforts to understand the dynamics of the therapy session are immediately focused on the therapist-client interaction; what the therapist said, how it was said, how the patient reacted. As we will see later, these issues are indeed important. However, a number of social psychological theories suggest that events preceeding the first therapy session are critical in determining the outcome of the therapy. Let us examine a few of those presession factors and the ways in which they might influence the progress of therapy.

*The importance of choice.*    Looking at the opening example, we find that John had to make a number of decisions regarding therapy even before he entered the psychologist's office. He made the important decision to enter therapy. Then, even though experiencing some conflict, John made the decision to call the psychologist and arrange for the initial meeting. He freely agreed to the initial appointment despite the fact that it meant rejecting other attractive alternatives such as playing softball. We also find that the psychologist was careful to allow John to make the decision about continuing the therapy. Thus, John had the cognition "I chose to enter therapy and I also chose to continue with the therapy after the first session." We may ask what the consequences were for John of making these decisions rather than having them made for him.

One of the basic principles of human behavior that underlies many social psychological theories is the notion of **consistency**. People strive for consistency in their lives.

They want the people they like to like them. They work to keep their attitudes consistent over time; an individual who voted for Democratic candidates this year is likely to vote for Democrats next year. Not only do individuals strive for consistency in their own lives, they also expect others to be consistent. We expect that someone who likes us today will also like us tomorrow unless the situation changes drastically. We expect someone who makes an appointment with us to keep that appointment. This expectation of consistency allows us to order and predict our world. People who do not act consistently are labeled "irrational" or "frivolous" and those people are often avoided.

Leon Festinger (1957) developed the theory of **cognitive dissonance** on the principle of consistency. Festinger defined cognition as a "piece of knowledge" about an attitude, a behavior, a value, or an emotion. For example, the fact that you like rye bread may be one of your cognitions. Another cognition may be the fact that you own a 1967 Ford. Everyone holds numerous cognitions simultaneously.

Festinger stated that cognitions can be related in two ways. They can be in a consonant relationship where one cognition follows from the other. For example, the cognition that you like roses is consonant with the cognition that you just planted two hundred rose bushes in your yard. On the other hand, cognitions can be related in a dissonant manner; this occurs when the opposite of one cognition follows from the other. Thus, the cognition that you hate large cities is dissonant with the cognition that you chose to live in Manhattan.

According to Festinger, people strive to hold consonant cognitions. When an individual finds that he holds cognitions in a dissonant relationship, he will experience an unpleasant psychological state labeled "cognitive dissonance." When this happens, the individual will become motivated to reduce the dissonance by altering one or both of the cognitions to achieve a state of consonance. Thus, consonance can be restored to the above example about large cities if you were to decide that you really enjoy large cities. This cognition is then consonant with the fact that you chose to live in Manhattan.

Festinger and others (e.g., Brehm and Cohen, 1962; Wicklund and Brehm, 1977) point out that cognitive dissonance nearly always results when an individual makes a decision. When we make a decision we are committing ourselves to one alternative and rejecting another one. The more attractive the rejected alternative, the greater the dissonance; the cognition that I rejected alternative A is dissonant with the fact that alternative A is attractive. One way to reconcile this dissonance is to reduce the attractiveness of alternative A and increase the value of the alternative I have chosen. Thus, consonance is restored when I can say that I chose an attractive alternative and rejected an unattractive one. Hence, following a decision, dissonance theory postulates that there will be a tendency to enhance the value of the chosen alternative and reduce the value of the rejected alternative.

One further point should be noted in understanding the conditions that give rise to dissonance. This is that the individual must see himself or herself as having freely made a decision before dissonance will result. If the individual feels forced to accept one alternative, no dissonance will follow and there will not be the motivation to enhance the value of the received alternative. This results because the cognition that I was forced to take alternative B is not dissonant with either the cognition that alternative B is not attractive or that alternative A is attractive.

Thus, we have dissonance theory that postulates that because of people's desire for consistency, they attempt to enhance the value of alternatives that they freely choose and reduce the value of alternatives they reject. We may now ask the question, How does this apply to the example of the therapy session that opened this chapter? As we pointed out earlier, John had numerous cognitions involving his entering therapy. He chose to begin therapy; he made the initial appointment; he chose to continue therapy.

Given these cognitions, we can see the direction that

the drive for consistency would push John's attitudes. It would be inconsistent and arouse cognitive dissonance for John to hold the congitions "I freely chose to enter therapy even though it will not help me." The consonant set of cognitions are that John chose to enter therapy and he believes that it will help him. Viewing the situation from John's point of view, we see that he cannot alter the cognition that he has chosen to enter therapy; he did make the appointment and is sitting in the therapist's office. Thus, he cannot alter his behavior but he can change his attitudes to become consonant with his behavior.

Dissonance theory, then, argues strongly for allowing the client to feel that he or she has made the decision to enter and to continue with therapy. As a result of the perception of having freely chosen to enter and continue therapy, the client should be motivated to value and believe in the efficacy of the treatment. The client who feels forced into therapy has little motivation to view it in a positive light.

*Effort.*   Oftentimes there is a tendency to tailor therapy sessions to the client's convenience and desires. Scheduling may be worked out so that the therapy session does not conflict with anything else that the client wishes to do. Fees may be set so that they do not cause any financial burden on the client. In some cases, transportation may be arranged so that the client has door-to-door service. Certainly it is important to ensure that a therapy program causes no undue hardships on the client. However, according to a number of social psychological studies, the "bending-over-backwards" approach may not have the desired beneficial effects on the client.

In an interesting study, Aronson and Mills (1959) invited female college students to participate in group discussions on sex. The women were told that before they could participate they must undergo a screening test in order to ensure that they would be able to contribute to the discussion. Some of the subjects were placed in the Severe Initiation condition; they had to read a list of very obscene words and recite a lucid passage describing sexual activity. Another group was placed in the Mild Initiation condition; they read a list of rather innocuous sex-related words. The final group of subjects served as the control group and were given no screening test.

TABLE 1    Relationship Between Severity of Initiation and Attraction for the Group

| OBJECT OF RATING | EXPERIMENTAL CONDITION | | |
|---|---|---|---|
| | Control | Mild Initiation | Severe Initiation |
| Discussion | 80.2[1] | 81.8 | 97.6 |
| Participants | 89.9 | 89.3 | 97.7 |

[1] The higher the number the more positive the rating.
Adapted from Aronson and Mills (1959), p. 179.

Following the initiations, all subjects listened to a group discussion on "the secondary sex behavior of lower animals." Subjects were led to believe that the discussants were members of the group that they would soon join. After listening to the discussion, subjects were asked to rate how interesting they found the discussion. As can be seen from the results presented in Table 1, subjects who underwent the severe initiation were more attracted to the group than were subjects who were in the mild initiation or control conditions. It is important to note that all subjects listened to the same "group discussion" and, therefore, the differences in the ratings were caused by the severity of the initiation.

How can these results be explained? This study and a number of similar ones (e.g., Schooler and Bateson, 1962; Gerard and Mathewson, 1966) were designed to test the prediction from dissonance theory that we love those things for which we suffer. The cognitions that I worked hard and suffered to obtain an object of little value are dissonant. In the Aronson and Mills experiment, it would create cognitive dissonance for the subjects to hold the cognitions "I just went through this terribly difficult and embarrassing ordeal to join a dull and uninteresting group." The subjects could not change the fact that they had, indeed, worked hard to get into the discussion group. They could, however, justify this work and reduce dissonance by enhancing the value of the group. Thus, the cognitions that I worked hard to join an interesting group are consonant. The women in the mild initiation group should not have suffered dissonance since the cognitions that "I put in little work to join an uninteresting group" are not dissonant. Thus, dissonance theory hypothesizes that we value those things for which we suffer.

Applying this proposition to therapy, it is suggested that the therapy session should not be designed to provide the maximum convenience for the client. The client who must work to get into the therapy session should value it more than the one who does not. In the opening example, we see that John had to decide to forego playing softball to keep his appointment for therapy. He also had to make the commitment to pay his hard-earned money to continue the therapy sessions. In order to justify these efforts, John would have to hold high expectations for the efficacy of the session. As we will see in the next section, having the client hold high expectations for the outcome of therapy is an important step toward successful treatment.

*The role of expectations.* Casey Stengal, a famous baseball manager, once remarked "The most talented player in the world is not worth a damn to me unless he has the attitude that he can win." Stengal was referring to the fact that a baseball team loaded with talent may not have a winning record unless the players believe and expect to win. In social psychology, a similar phenomenon is referred to as the **self-fulfilling prophecy**. This term is used to describe the situation where an individual expects something to happen and unwittingly influences events so that the expectancy is confirmed.

A clear example of the self-fulfilling prophecy was found by Rosenthal and Jacobson (1968). They told elementary school teachers that "reliable tests had indicated" that certain children in their classroom should show dramatic increases in academic achievement over the year. In actuality, no tests had been given and the "certain children" were chosen at random. However, the manipulation had created the expectation with the teachers that these children would perform well. I.Q. tests taken at the end of the school year indicated that the prophecy was fulfilled; those children who had been designated as high achievers showed more than twice the improvement in I. Q. as did the control group of children who were in the same classroom but had not been designated as high achievers. Scrutiny of the teachers' behaviors over the year suggested that they may have unwittingly been responsible for this self-fulfilling prophecy. In some cases they paid special attention to "high achievers"; they often rewarded the high achievers for behaviors that went unrewarded in the control children.

The important point to note is that the outcome was affected by the expectations of the teachers. Much the same process can occur in therapy. The client who does not expect to improve through therapy is unlikely to improve, while the individual who expects the therapy "to work" is more likely to improve. The expectations can be confirmed in subtle ways. The client who believes that therapy will reduce his tenseness may notice that he falls asleep more quickly one night than on past nights. He may then say to himself that the therapy is beginning to be successful. This feeling itself may result in more relaxation and further feelings of satisfaction with the therapy. On the other hand, the client who does not expect the therapy to be successful may notice the same behavior but attribute it to the fact that "he was just more tired than normal."

We can note the role of expectations in the opening

example. The effort John went through to enter therapy should have resulted in some expectations that the therapy would be successful. Further, as the sessions progressed, the therapist worked to instill further expectations of the efficacy of the therapy. He allowed John to believe that the improvements in his behavior were due to the therapy and these beliefs further enhanced John's expectations.

### Therapist-Client Interactions

While we have been focusing on pretherapy events, it is obvious that factors that occur in the therapy session are vital in determining the success of therapy. It is highly unlikely that a client will "open up" to a therapist he or she does not like or trust. Likewise, a client who is made to feel little control over his or her own behavior in the therapy session is likely to obtain very little long-term help from the sessions. Since the therapy session involves interpersonal interaction between the psychologist and client, there are a number of social psychological theories of relevance.

*Interpersonal attraction.* It is important that there be some degree of attraction between the client and therapist. It is unlikely that a client will work hard for improvement if he or she is not comfortable with the psychologist. The client may actually work against rather than work with a therapist who is disliked. Taking this a step further, it is probable that the client will terminate therapy if dislike for the therapist continues. The therapist's attraction to the client comprises the other side of the coin. The issue is not often raised but it is not hard to see that a therapist is likely to have some difficulty working with a client he or she dislikes. Thus, the issue of interpersonal attraction is an important one for understanding the dynamics of therapy.

There are a number of social psychological theories dealing with the topic of interpersonal attraction. One of the most researched theories states that we are attracted to those who are similar to us (Byrne, 1971). Further, the greater the number and more important the dimensions of similarity, the greater the attraction. It is interesting to note that similarity in almost any area leads to increased liking. For example, Byrne, Clore, and Worchel (1966) found that similarity on economic conditions leads to increased attraction, while Senn (1971) found that individuals who viewed themselves of similar ability responded with greater liking. In fact, the only dimension on which similarity does not seem to enchance attraction is on personality characteristics (Byrne, Griffitt, and Stenfaniak, 1967).

Looking at the opening example, we can see how perceived similarity may well have increased John's liking of Frank. John felt he had something in common with Frank in that they both liked the same types of magazines and both were amateur photographers. In this case, the similarity in age between John and Frank may also have been a factor leading to increased interpersonal attraction. Certainly, we do not mean to imply that age differences or sex differences between therapist and client will mitigate against a successful therapeutic relationship. We simply wish to point out that similarities on these dimensions may play a part in increasing attraction toward the therapist.

Another factor affecting interpersonal attraction is proximity. We have all heard the saying "absence makes the heart grow fonder." Research, however, suggests that the opposite is more often true; familiarity breeds attraction. In an early study, Bossard (1932) examined 5,000 marriage license applications in Philadelphia. He found a strong inverse relationship between the number of applications and the distance between the homes of the engaged individuals—the greater the distance the less likely was an application for a marriage license. Investigations have repeatedly found that friendships are most likely to occur between individuals who live close together and see each other often (e.g., Festinger, Schachter, and Back, 1950; Byrne, 1961).

Similarly, Zajonc (1968) reported a mere exposure phenomenon; people like those people and objects that they have most contact with. Zajonc showed subjects a number of photographs; they saw some of the photographs more often than others. He later asked subjects how much they liked the people in the photographs. Even though all the people depicted were strangers, subjects reported being more attracted to those people whose pictures they had seen most often.

These findings are interesting in light of questions about how often clients should have contact with their psychologist. We see that John scheduled regular sessions with Frank over a long period of time. It is highly likely that the large amount of contact led to increased attraction between the two. Thus, one of the results of frequent sessions may be increased interpersonal attraction between client and therapist.

Another model of attraction states that we like people who reward us or are associated with rewards (Lott and Lott, 1968). This model offers two distinct predictions. The first is that we like people who do nice things for us. In the case of the therapy session, this model suggests that the client should become increasingly attracted to the therapist as difficult problems are worked through. In this case the therapist can be seen as directly rewarding the client by helping to provide solutions to problems. Even further, much of the therapy session involves the therapist rewarding the client for attempting to work on problems. In the sessions between Frank and John, the therapist continually rewarded the client by statements such as "That's good," "I think you are moving along fine," "That's very interesting." The effect of this positive approach should be not only that the client continues to work on the problems but that he becomes more comfortable with and attracted to the therapist.

Looking at the dynamics of this situation from another angle, we could also predict that the therapist becomes more attracted to the client who rewards him. In this case, the rewards may come in the form of insights by the client or willingness on the part of the client to discuss areas that had heretofore been taboo. Hence, the direct reward system in therapy is a two-way street.

The second prediction of the reward model is that we like people who are around us when good things happen. This effect occurs even when those people are not in any way responsible for the pleasant event. For example, Veitch and Griffitt (1976) had subjects listen to a radio program that reported either good or bad news. Immediately after the program, a stranger entered the room. When subjects were subsequently asked to rate the stranger, the results indicated that he was liked more when he appeared after the good news than after the bad news. Thus, simply being associated with a pleasant or unpleasant event affected attraction.

This situation often occurred in the therapy session with Frank and John. Frank provided John a forum in which to explore his problem and the possible root of the problem. In the first session, Frank simply listened as John explored the conditions that led up to the incident in the supermarket. Through this self-exploration, John began to see how his relationship with his father may have contributed to the incident. This insight was a very pleasant experience for John. Interestingly, even though John essentially worked through to this conclusion on his own, his attraction for Frank increased because of Frank's association with this pleasant experience.

Thus, there are a number of factors that contribute to the attraction between the client and therapist. Some are obvious while others are not. However, in the case of Frank and John, all these factors contributed to the growing bond between the two and to the eventual success of the therapy.

*Trust.*    Many of the therapy sessions between Frank and John involved attempts to establish trust. In the first session, John was wary and distrustful of Frank. He was guarded and "opened up" very little. As the sessions continued, John tested Frank. He broached sensitive areas; he made statements that he thought would shock or anger Frank. Each time he watched Frank's response. Frank accepted these tests and behaved in an encouraging, helpful manner. He refused to "match wits" or be drawn into a competitive interaction with John. Slowly John came to trust Frank. As time progressed he felt freer to discuss sensitive topics and to make himself more vulnerable. His openess was now aimed at achieving a resolution to his problem rather than testing Frank. The trust he developed for Frank served as a catalyst for progress and eventually allowed him to find the solution he sought.

The term *trust* is often used when referring to therapy. There seems to be almost total agreement that trust between client and therapist is necessary if therapy is to be successful. However, there is disagreement about exactly what trust is or how it develops.

The concept of trust is utilized in social psychological studies of conflict and conflict resolution. The importance of trust in conflict resolution is clearly demonstrated in the Prisoner's Dilemma (Luce and Raiffe, 1957). Imagine the situation where the police have captured two persons they believe have committed a murder. The district attorney, however, does not believe that he has enough evidence to convict the two of a murder charge. The only way in which he can win a murder verdict against them is for at least one of them to turn state's evidence and confess. In an attempt to achieve this end, the district attorney places the two men in separate prison cells where they can neither see nor communicate with each other. The D. A. enters the cell of each inmate separately and outlines a proposition. He explains, however, that he does not have enough evidence to convict the prisoners of murder, which carries a ninety-nine-year sentence. He explains that he does have enough evidence to convict the prisoners of robbery, which carries a five-year sentence. He then offers to make a deal; if the prisoner will turn state's evidence and confess to the murder, the confessor will be given a very light sentence (1 year) and the nonconfessor will have "the book thrown at him" (99 years). However, if both confess, they will receive moderate sentences for the murder (15 years).

It should be remembered that the two prisoners cannot communicate with each other but each is aware that his partner has been offered the same deal. It is clear that from the standpoint of both prisoners, the best response is for neither to confess; in this case they both get a relatively light sentence. However, if the inmates believe that their partner will "double cross" them and confess, a confession becomes the safest response. The point of the Prisoner's Dilemma that has fascinated social psychologists is that the decision of each party must be based on the trust felt for the other party. If A trusts B not to confess, he has two options; he can make the response best for the pair (not confess) or best for himself (confess). However, if he does not trust B, he must confess. Situations such as this indicate the vital role trust plays in conflict reduction.

Trust has been defined as the expectancy that another will act in a helpful rather than hurtful way (Pruitt, 1965). A number of investigators (e.g., Schlenker, Helm, and Tedeschi, 1973; Zand, 1972) have found that trust develops when one individual runs the risk of letting down his guard and making himself vulnerable to see if the other abuses this vulnerability. Trust develops slowly only after many such "tests."

On the other hand, distrust is quickly established. Worchel (1979) observed that "it may take only one betrayal to establish distrust" and "once aroused, distrust is extremely resistive to change." The difficulty in eliminating distrust occurs because the betrayed individual becomes unwilling to chance further vulnerability and, hence, steps toward reestablishing trust are not taken. Worchel (1979) reports that trust may be rebuilt if the transgressor admits the betrayal and convinces the wronged individual that he is truly remorseful for the action.

*Attribution of emotions.*   Throughout the opening example are instances where John reported "feeling" emotions. He reported feeling excitement, fear, attraction, anger, happiness, confusion, and panic during different periods in the therapy. It is interesting and important to note that the particular emotion that John "felt" determined how he responded during the therapy session. In the first session, when John perceived that he was fearful, he became cautious and avoided starting a conversation with Frank. Similarly, in the third session, John's happiness motivated him to "open up" and discuss sensitive issues. He responded to the happiness by suggesting holding an additional session that week.

It may not be a startling revelation that our emotions play a role in dictating our behavior. This point, however, is particulary important to understand when viewing the therapy session. Each session is relatively short in duration and the tone of the session may be set rather early by the emotional state of the client. This discussion suggests that it is important to understand how individuals experience emotions.

On the face of it, a discussion of the way in which we experience emotions may seem unnecessary; an event causes us to feel a particular way (aroused) and that feeling determines our emotion. While this may be the popular position even today, investigators have determined that this is not necessarily the way in which individuals experience emotions. The body is capable of only a limited number of types of arousal, while individuals experience an almost unlimited variety of emotions. Hence, the particular arousal cannot determine the individual's emotional state.

In 1892, William James hypothesized that emotions have two components—affective (arousal) and cognitive. According to James, an individual becomes aroused, responds to the arousal, and then seeks to explain the arousal. The explanation becomes the emotion. James used the following example to illustrate his point: we see a bear, then experience a physiological arousal. We then run. In determining our emotion, we review the events (arousal and running) and then label our emotion (fear). Thus, according to James one of the determinants of our emotion is our response to an event.

In 1962 Schachter and Singer revised James' theory. They, too, hypothesized that emotions have a physiological and cognitive component. They believed that the label an individual places on an emotion could either be determined by his own response or cues from the environment (e.g., the actions of other people). Essentially, they suggested that an individual becomes aroused and then searches the immediate environment to determine the reason for the arousal. The reason the individual decides upon determines the particular emotion. The implication of this theory is that the same physiological arousal may lead to the experience of very different emotions since the particular type of emotion is determined by the environmental cues rather than the type of arousal.

In a clever experiment Schachter and Singer (1962) told subjects that they were taking part in a study on the effects of a vitamin supplement (Suproxin). The subjects received an injection of the "vitamin" and were then told that they would have to wait for the drug to take effect. Some of the subjects were told nothing about the expected effect of the injection (ignorant); others were told that the injection would cause them to feel aroused and excited (informed). Actually the injection contained epinephrine, which would arouse and excite the subjects. Following these explanations, subjects were placed in a waiting room with another "subject." This other subject was actually an experimental confederate. In some cases the confederate began acting euphoric, dancing around the room and making paper airplanes. In other conditions, the confederate acted angry and agitated and tore up a questionnaire given to him by the experimenter. After a few minutes, the experimenter returned and asked the subjects to describe their emotional states.

The results showed that the confederate's behavior strongly affected the subjects' descriptions of their emotions in the ignorant condition but not in the informed condition. In the ignorant condition, subjects with the happy confederate reported being happy and euphoric while subjects with the angry confederate reported being angry. The subjects' emotions did not mimic the confederate's behavior when subjects knew the reason for their arousal. Schachter and Singer explained their result by saying that subjects in the ignorant condition were aroused but did not know the reason for their arousal. They therefore utilized environmental cues (the confederate's behavior) to label their emotion. Subjects in the informed condition knew why they were aroused and hence did not need the additional cues to label their emotion. The interesting point of the study is that subjects in the ignorant conditions experienced the same arousal but reported very different emotions depending on the environmental cues.

Thus, the research demonstrates that an individual's emotions may be determined by the actions of other people in his or her environment. The reader may have experienced the phenomenon of going through a day where a number of people remarked, "You don't look so well today." While you may have felt fine upon waking in the morning, you actually "feel ill" by late afternoon after a score of people have told you that you look ill.

Returning to the therapy session example, we can hypothesize that Frank's behavior could have affected the labels John placed on his emotions. In the first session, Frank's casual remark for John not to feel fearful may have suggested to John that the knots in his stomach were because he was actually feeling fear. He must be feeling fear if Frank could pick it up. In the third session when John again felt the knots in his stomach, Frank's comment "You're smiling today; you must be happy" may have helped John determine that his arousal was happiness and excitement. This label was reinforced when John saw Frank laughing and smiling throughout the session.

Thus, another means by which Frank dictated the direction of the sessions was in the giving of cues that helped determine the label John would place on his arousal.

## Summary

Theories of social psychology are relevant both to events that take place before the therapy session and to the dynamics of the therapy session. The theory of cognitive dissonance predicts that the individual will feel more committed to the therapy and be more likely to continue with it if he has freely made the choice to enter therapy. In such cases, he will have to justify his decision and one justification is to believe that the therapy will be beneficial Cognitive dissonance theory also suggests that the more effort an individual expends in making a decision, the more committed he will be to that decision. The expectations an individual has about therapy also affect the likelihood of successful treatment. Research has shown that individuals often unwittingly behave in a manner designed to fulfill their expectations.

The degree of attraction between client and therapist will influence the outcome of the sessions. Social psychologists have found that a number of factors affect attraction. Individuals are generally attracted to those who are perceived as being similar to them. Attraction also results from simple physical proximity. Finally, research has found that individuals are attracted to people who provide rewards or positive situations. Because the therapy session involves the client revealing personal and private information, the issue of trust between client and therapist is important. Trust develops through risk-taking behavior and while it often takes a great deal of time for a trusting relationship to result, distrust may follow one act of betrayal. Throughout the therapy session, the client will experience a number of emotions. Schachter has shown that an emotion results from a physiological arousal followed by an attribution about the cause of that arousal.

## APPLICATIONS IN CLINICAL PRACTICE

It seems clear from the above section that choice, consistency, dissonance, effort, expectation, attraction, trust and attribution all play some part in the conduct and effectiveness of psychotherapy. As might be expected, some therapies and therapy techniques may intentionally or unintentionally capitalize on some or all of these considerations to promote effective therapy. Each type of therapy may employ a different constellation of these social psychological forces. Below, some common schools of therapy will be reviewed and then discussed in terms of how they employ the social psychological phenomena. It is important to state that there is much more to each therapy than just the effect attributable to social psychological forces, but these forces are in many cases essential to the understanding of the efficacy of that therapy.

## Behavior Therapies

*Overview.* The major principle of behavior therapy is that all behavior, adaptive or maladaptive, is learned. That process follows certain principles of learning developed by experimental and learning psychologists. To change behavior the learned responses need to be unlearned and more appropriate or effective responses learned. The backbones of all behavior techniques are the concepts of learning: classical conditioning, operant conditioning, and observational learning.

Classical conditioning as a phenomenon was first discovered by Pavlov. He found that an unconditioned stimulus (such as the presentation of food powder to a hungry dog) elicited an unconditioned response (salivation). If the unconditioned stimulus was paired with a previously neutral stimulus (the ringing of a bell), it would eventually elicit the same response the unconditioned stimulus produced even when no longer paired with that unconditioned stimulus. The conditioned stimulus would then produce a conditioned response which was formerly the unconditioned response. The dog, for instance, would then salivate at the sound of the bell without the presentation of the food powder. In a more clinical example, John might become anxious when presented with a neutral stimulus which had in the past been paired with another stimulus that produced anxiety. If, for instance, when he was about six years old John had been eating a turkey dinner when his parents had a terrible argument, the mere appearance of a turkey dinner might now elicit the anxiety reaction he had when he was forced to watch his parents fighting.

Our understanding of operant or instrumental conditioning is based upon the work of E. L. Thorndike and his followers. According to this theory, behavior which is followed by a rewarding consequence is more likely to occur in the future given the same situation, while behavior which is punished, negatively reinforced, or ignored is less likely to occur in the same situation again. In John's case, it might be that he was rewarded for appearing anxious in a particular situation. When in that situation again, he would repeat the behavior to gain the reward or to avoid punishment.

The third major principle is observational learning. Bandura (1969) and his coworkers discovered that responses can be learned by simply observing others. This type of learning from a model is called "modeling." The behavior of another *and* its consequences are observed and then later performed by the observer. In John's case it may be that he once saw someone severely punished for not being anxious or rewarded for showing that response. He then performs that response in the similar situation even though he has never responded in that way before.

Most behavioral therapy techniques address one of the above principles and attempt to promote the learning of adaptive responses to replace those which were not adaptive. Among the most common of the techniques are systematic desensitization, aversive counterconditioning, flooding, operant conditioning, and modeling.

Systematic desensitization or reciprocal inhibition was first explored by Wolpe (1958). It is based upon the idea that two competing responses such as anxiety and relaxation cannot occur simultaneously. The procedure involves training the client to relax on command and then gradually pairing that relaxation with increasingly anxiety-provoking images until no anxiety is experienced. In John's case, the treatment might proceed as follows: John is taught how to relax and asked to visualize a scene while relaxed (for instance lying on the beach). He is then asked to construct an anxiety hierarchy of items of increasing anxiety to him. The lowest item might be thinking about going to the grocery store and the highest item standing in a crowd of people staring at him. Starting with the least anxiety-provoking item, John would be asked to relax and then visualize the scene on his hierarchy while remaining relaxed. If he cannot do this he will be asked to relax and then try again until he can see himself thinking of going to the store without experiencing anxiety. Then he would proceed up the hierarchy until he could imagine the most anxiety-producing event while being relaxed. At this point he can no longer be anxious. It is important to note that in the use of this technique, visualization seems to be quite effective and if the client can visualize the scene without anxiety he or she is likely to be without anxiety in that situation in real life.

Aversive counterconditioning therapy involves pairing the object or undesirable behavior with an aversive stimulus such as electric shock. If you were trying to lose weight, for instance, you might be presented with pictures of fattening food and then receive a mild shock or a punishment of some kind.

Operant conditioning would involve rewarding you for positive changes in behavior, such as paying you for losing weight. In this case the reinforcement for the appropriate behavior is given. It does mean that the person must be capable of emitting that behavior or something close to that behavior in order to receive the reinforcement.

Flooding or implosion techniques involve extinguishing the maladaptive response by subjecting the person to massive amounts of anxiety for a long period of time until they learn that the consequence they fear, the one that is making them anxious, does not occur. If the therapist believed that John's anxiety was caused by a fear, he would place John in the fear-producing situation for a long period of time until John is convinced that the thing he fears does not occur. If we use the sample of the turkey and argument, the therapist would have John imagine eating a turkey dinner and demonstrate to him that no argument ensues. Implosion and flooding often exaggerate the fear situation to speed up the process.

Finally, modeling is the process of watching a model perform the adaptive behavior and having the client see the consequences. In some cases the therapist serves as the model for the client of how to deal with the problem. In some cases the client will choose another model. This technique may use role-playing, where the client can rehearse the adaptive responses while modeling another person.

*Social psychological factors.*     Of the therapies discussed above, the most commonly used are those based upon reinforcement or what might be called contingency. The idea of contingency is clearly related to that of expectation. Changing or clarifying contingencies (if I do this then that will happen) is a way of establishing an expectation about the future based upon the past. Behavior therapies make clear to the client that by setting forth specific contingencies, certain things will be expected. This relates not only to relearning the behavior in question, but also to what might be expected from therapy. Behavior therapists frequently emphasize the predictable and concrete steps in therapy in order to create the expectation in the client that treatment and outcome (in this case contingency) will also be quite predictable. This may create in the client the expectation of success which may in turn serve as an aid in treatment. In the case of reciprocal inhibition techniques such as systematic desensitization, the steps in the desensitization hierarchy traditionally paired with the relaxation response serve to desensitize the client to increasingly anxiety-provoking stimuli and may have the additional effect of allowing the client to experience some success in reducing anxiety along the way. This success may in turn create a general expectation of success which will aid in reducing anxiety farther up the hierarchy.

In addition to using expectations, behavior therapies also make use of effort and choice. Clients participate actively in defining the behaviors to be changed, in constructing hierarchies, etc. This should create a feeling that they are choosing certain aspects of the treatment and this may increase their level of commitment to it. This "involvement" in the process of therapy may create positive results as clients justify to themselves the "choice"of the therapy they have made. The entire process of choosing also requires the expenditure of effort by the client. Effort may also be expended in doing homework assignments. The more the clients participate in the therapy the more direct effort they may see themselves giving and the more may be invested in making the therapy successful. This may than allow the therapy to be more successful.

Cognitive dissonance will also facilitate the client's motivation in therapy. If the person chooses to be in therapy, he must begin to assume that it is because he believes that it will be effective or that he likes it, otherwise he would not be doing it. If this is the case, he will then have a positive attitude toward the therapy and continue to work in that setting.

Effort justification may also help the client if the treatment seems particularly stressful, as in the case of flooding or implosion. The more effort expended, the more investment in success. Also role playing may allow the client to feel that effort is being expended. The role playing of desired responses in problem situations can be helpful by allowing the person not only to experience a lifelike scene, but also to expend effort in actively participating in the therapy session. In addition, role playing may create the expectation of success in the client if the scene is played to a desired positive conclusion. Effort may also be a function of the fee that the client pays. To the extent that the client must expend effort to earn or procure money, spending the money on therapy may represent the expenditure of effort; the more effort the more justification required.

Other "cognitive" behavior therapies such as Rational Emotive Therapy (Ellis, 1958) and Cognitive Behavior Therapy (Michenbaum, 1977) may ask the client to indulge in some cognitive "self-talk." This self-talk usually involves the client reciting statements subvocally when encountering the problem situation. Such a procedure may help the person clarify the expectations of the situation and actively expend effort to deal with it. Again the effort and the expectation created for the client in working with the therapist may affect how successful he or she will be in dealing with the problem responses. Perhaps, most important, the self-talk or cognitive analysis will force the person to set aside some of the expectations that the situation may be a problem by being specific about what exactly is being encountered and how to deal with it. This may reduce the effect of previous negative expectations and create positive ones.

In general, behavioral therapies rely heavily upon choice, expectation, effort justification, and dissonance in their treatment regimens. Interpersonal attraction between the therapist and the client, although important, is not essential for behavior therapy. Most behavior therapies are specific in terms of technique and do not employ personal attraction as a motivating force. Rather they tend to count more heavily upon rationality, logic, and the manipulation of expectations. These therapies encourage a good therapist-client relationship, but attraction is not necessary.

It is not surprising that behavior therapies seem to be quite effective in the treatment of phobias. Phobias are usually considered to be irrational fears. In other words, a person fears the phobic object even though the expectation of harm is not rational under normal circumstances. A person with a fear of dogs, for instance, may fear that all dogs will bite him, and further, the fear is generalized to assume that dogs may be present in places where rationally or logically they do not frequently appear. A behavioral treatment of such a condition will result in changing the expectation that dogs will appear by allowing the person to reduce his anxiety enough to actually encounter the dog and not be bitten. Prior to the therapy the fear could not be disproven because the person was too anxious to even encounter the object. Once the dog can be encountered, the fear can be disproven logically and clients can alter their expectations concerning their next feared encounter with a canine. This will allow for the learning of a new response in the presence of a dog and the creation of a new expectation. Since these sorts of therapies are good at addressing specific expectations, often based upon prior learning and expectation, they are most effective with phobias and neurotic responses to specific objects and/or circumstances.

## Psychodynamic Therapies

*Overview.* Psychodynamic theory assumes that psychological problems are a result of unsolved emotional difficulties that occurred in early childhood. The therapy must create for the patient a corrective emotional experience. This experience would serve to correct the previously unresolved emotional problem. In order to accomplish this, the therapist must engender in the patient some emotional feeling in the session. This is usually most effectively accomplished through the process of transference. Transference takes place when the patient responds to the therapist as a parent. It is believed that almost all later difficulty for the patient is a result of some unresolved feeling toward one or both parents. Once the transference occurs, the therapist may deal with the patient's feelings toward the parent directly as an object of those feelings. Most psychodynamically-oriented psychotherapists endeavor to be a "blank screen" onto which the patient projects the image of the parent. Then the process of reexperiencing and untangling the unresolved Oedipal feelings may begin. It is these feelings that are believed to be the cause of neurosis.

Psychodynamic therapies range from short-term therapy to long-term psychoanalysis. In each case the immediate goals of therapy may be different, but the assumptions used by the therapist to reach the goals are the same. The corrective emotional experience must take place or at least be attempted. The process of psychoanalysis is long and complicated but considered as essential in order to produce the desired lasting changes in the patient. Short-term therapies are sometimes considered to be the best treatment when time is limited.

Within psychodynamic therapy there are a variety of different techniques. All such therapies share the assumption that the person's difficulty is related to some unconscious forces. The goal of therapy is to expose these forces through the process of transference, bring them into therapy, and resolve the difficulties they have caused.

*Social psychological factors.* Although psychodynamic therapists are trained to be the objects of transference and to deal with their own transference with the patients (countertransference), more than in any other part of the therapy, personal attraction and personal perception between therapist and patient is important. Most especially in the case of the patient or client, initial feelings toward the therapist may greatly influence the outcome of therapy as well as how rapidly it may proceed. In the case of transference, however, it is not only the attraction the patient may feel but the negative feelings as well. These negative feelings may make it more difficult for the patient in the beginning to relate to the therapist but ultimately may be more important in establishing the transference. Depending upon how one views the construction of personality, the personal relationship between the patient and the therapist may be more important than just for the purposes of establishing the transference.

Neo-Freudians, most notably Harry Stack Sullivan, believed that the interpersonal relationship of the patient and therapist was significant as an example of the patient's relationships with other people beside the parents. Sullivan (1953) saw therapy as an interpersonal event. He changed the traditional Freudian therapy (psychoanalysis) by having the patient and therapist sit facing each other rather than having the patient on the couch and the therapist sitting out of sight taking notes. For Sullivan, the attraction and positive feeling passed between the two parties in the office was an essential part of effective therapy. The more the patient could like and relate to the therapist personally, the more chance for success in therapy.

In addition to attraction, expectation plays a central role in psychodynamic therapy. In psychoanalysis, one of the first steps taken is setting up the "analytic compact" between the patient and the therapist (in this case the analyst). This compact is usually an agreement that the patient will attempt not to censor any material he would tell. In return, the analyst will not be judgmental of the patient. Also, strict rules about attendance at therapy, scheduling of sessions, and payment of fees are established by the analyst. All of these procedures serve to establish an expectation in the patient that the therapist or the analyst is in control of the treatment. To many patients this may be a powerful influence for the good as they wish someone forcefully to take control of the problems they face so that they may be solved. For some individuals, however, the idea of giving up some control may be difficult and may motivate them to leave therapy prematurely before they can reassert their own control with the help of the therapist. In John's case the therapist set specific rules about fees and attendance. Some patients may opt for a different form of therapy, while others may not seek therapy at all on the basis of the expectation that they may have to give up some control. Individual cases may be positively or negatively affected by the patient's expectations of the therapy and the therapist.

Therapy with John would center upon his relationship with his father and his unresolved feeling toward him. The therapist would attempt to facilitate transference, at which time John would begin to show the same feelings toward Frank that he had shown his father. Once the feelings had been made conscious and expressed with Frank's help, John would begin to work them through. His relationship with Frank would need to be trusting and strong enough to survive the expression of negative feelings. Frank, for his part, would need to accept and make use of those feelings in the therapy. When John's feelings about his father and his unconscious desires and fears had been dealt with, according to psychodynamic theory, his anxiety in the problem situations would disappear.

The assumption of psychodynamic therapies, that behavior is a function of underlying psychodynamic forces, has traditionally been most effective with neurotic patients, especially those with pervasive or nonspecific difficulties in coping (as opposed to speciflc phobias or behavioral deficits). These problems are frequently manifest as problems of dealing with other people or with managing free-floating anxieties. It may be that psychodynamic therapies are made more effective because of the interpersonal force exerted between the therapist and the patient.

## Gestalt Therapy

*Overview.*   Gestalt therapy as first outlined and practiced by Fritz Perls (1958) involved extensive use of techniques focusing on the here and now experience of feelings. Clients are encouraged to talk about feelings they are experiencing in the therapy sessions, not what they have experienced in the past or expect to experience in the future. In addition, clients are asked to encounter parts of themselves or others portrayed in the imagination and seated in an "empty chair" in the consulting room. The therapist guides the client to experience fears and anxieties without needing to make cognitive "sense" of them. In that way expectations are not allowed to become more important in the therapy than the actual physical and emotional experience of the client. Experiencing the feelings first and then trying to label or understand them really may enable the client, with the help of the therapist, to examine the attributions he has made about the cause of the feelings and to, in some cases, relabel or make new attributions. The experience of anxiety, for instance, may be seen in Gestalt therapy as a pain in the stomach or breaking out in a cold sweat to which a label is attached. Just as in the Schachter and Singer (1962) study, arousal was labeled by some subjects as euphoria and as anger by others depending upon the social context in which they found themselves. In Gestalt therapy, emphasis is placed on examining the experience in the absence of the label. It is sometimes the labeling and not the experience which creates difficulty for the person in therapy. This approach also may aid the client in not being afraid of intense experience by becoming aware that experience is just sensation. It may be that the pain in the stomach is just arousal from some hot chili and not the anxiety attack it was labeled to be. In addition, the client learns that all sensation and experience is within oneself, not as a result of others.

*Social psychological factors.* Gestalt therapy may produce an increase in self-attributions which may produce more of a feeling of control in the client. Rather than being a victim of circumstance, the person is a receptor of sensation. If the experience can be felt and not cut off by the labeling process, it can be fully explored by the person and changes in the labeling of that experience become possible. In addition, clients may begin to "trust" their experience as not being right or wrong but just being. This means that responses were not necessarily wrong in the past, just not useful. In terms of the relationship with the therapist, the revealing of experience, and through that, vulnerability, can create a strong bond of trust between the two people in the consulting room, allowing for even fuller expression of feeling and more effective therapy.

Gestalt therapy with John would involve a here-and-now focus. Some of this approach was used by Frank in the example. John would be further encouraged to experience his feelings in the session, and to complete any "unfinished business" he might have had with his father. Frank might ask John to imagine his dead father in the empty chair and speak to him, expressing all of the feelings that he never had been able to express.

Gestalt therapies allow and facilitate the relabeling of experience and, therefore, seem quite effective for those either seemingly crippled by the pain of feelings (frequently situational adjustment reactions) as well as people out of touch with their feelings who may find their lives empty, incomplete, or dull (depressions of the situational kind). Also phobic fears can often be relabeled.

## Client-Centered Therapy

*Overview.* Client-centered therapy developed by Carl Rogers (1951) is based upon one major premise: that if the therapist presents the proper conditions to the client, the client will grow and change in the direction necessary to become self-actualized. For Rogers, the force toward this self-actualization is innate in all people. Therapy serves only to remove the barrier to its fulfillment. The therapist, in order to promote growth in the client, must demonstrate attitudes of congruence and acceptance, offer "unconditional positive regard," and demonstrate a great deal of empathy. This action by the therapist will allow the client to perceive himself in a different, more healthy, way which will promote change and growth toward self-actualization.

Unlike other techniques, client-centered therapy allows the client to determine what will transpire in sessions. The therapist plays a supportive role in helping the client to see himself accurately. The therapist offers the client support in an effort to allow the free expression of feeling and to facilitate the client creating the solution to the presenting problem.

*Social psychological factors.* In essence, client-centered therapy is based upon the classic trust relationship. Anything which will engender trust in the therapist-client interaction will facilitate success in therapy. In addition to trust, this form of relationship promotes feelings of attraction and more than any other type of treatment allows the client to feel that he or she has choice in therapy. Even the structure of the sessions is left up to the discretion of the client. He or she can count on support and acceptance from the therapist at all times. This acceptance may allow clients to feel in control of the therapy and of their own lives. By being accepted by another person (the therapist) while being in control of the sessions, the client may begin to believe that he can take a more active part in controlling his own life and still be accepted.

The focus of client-centered therapy with John would be to let him explore his feelings about himself, about what had happened, and for Frank to validate (as he did) that those feelings were acceptable and, indeed, that John was acceptable. As the relationship developed and became more open, John might spontaneously feel better and cope better with the situations which gave him trouble in the past.

## Communication Therapies

Communication therapies are those which focus on the process of the communication between client and therapist. Included in this group are theories of brief therapy put forth by Watzlawick, Weakland, and Fisch (1974), metacommunication therapies such as those described by Bandler and Grinder (1975), and hypnotherapies.

Perhaps more than any of the other therapies mentioned, these therapies reflect a basic set of social psychological assumptions about the nature of human communication. For them, communication takes place on many levels, verbally and nonverbally. The major task in therapy becomes clarification of how the person communicates with the environment and other people and how the responses of the environment to the person are interpreted. In the case of hypnotherapy, especially, suggestions are made by the therapist to the client. The suggestions may often be interpreted as magical. They are magical, however, only to the extent that they communicate to a person on a level which cannot be understood using one's usual strategies for viewing the world. Indeed, these magical endeavors represent merely a greater sensitivity on the part of the therapist to communicate to the person without his consciously being aware of it. How the therapist learns this skill is related to a set of clinical sensitivities developed in interaction with a particular client. They are mostly based upon observations of how the client represents the world and what his expectations are. The therapist then uses this information to communicate to the person on many levels using verbal and nonverbal suggestions, paradoxical injunctions, and examining not only the presenting problems, but the solutions which the clients have used which may in themselves be the problems. A person, for example, who fears the dark usually has difficulty not because of the fear, but rather as a result of the solution used to avoid the fear.

Communications theory and therapies attempt to influence and change the behavior of clients through altering and/or clarifying the process of how the person represents the world and communicates with it. The therapist often serves as no more than a translator for the client to become sensitive to the information being presented by others and the environment. These therapies are especially effective when the client has either strong resistance or strong expectations. This is true in the case of phobias or in solving problems by adjusting behavior such as to lose weight or stop smoking.

Working with John using this sort of therapy might begin with getting him in touch with what his anxiety might be communicating to him consciously or unconsciously, to explore that by exaggerating the symptoms or by communicating directly with his unconscious mind. This could be accomplished by hypnosis or "reframing" or a number of other communication techniques. It may turn out that anxiety is not the problem for John; it is merely the solution he has chosen to avoid having to deal with the problem. By changing or removing the solution, he might be able to experience or reexperience what the problem is. Then, strategies to solve the problem could be developed.

### Social Psychological Therapies

Although it appears that therapy has existed for a long time without acknowledging the role of social psychology, there appears to be at least two examples of social psychological theory being applied directly to the treatment of clinical cases.

Storms and Nisbett (1970) used attribution theory in the treatment of insomnia. They gave two groups of students who had trouble sleeping placebo pills (sugar pills). Subjects in one group were told that the pills might have the effect of making it difficult to fall asleep, while in the other they were told the pill would help them sleep. The results demonstrated that those who thought the pills would keep them up had little trouble sleeping while the other group continued to have difficulty. Storms and Nisbett observed that subjects in the first group believed that the pill would keep them up, so when they could not sleep, they attributed it to the pill, became relaxed, and fell asleep. Those who expected to get drowsy from the pill and still felt awake attributed the arousal to themselves and became more concerned about not sleeping, thereby staying up even more. The pills by themselves had no effect. The ability of one group to sleep, then, was due to the misattribution they made to the pill as being responsible for their sleeplessness.

In a second social psychological study, Cooper (1979) used cognitive dissonance to treat snake phobia. Subjects who were afraid of snakes volunteered to be in a room with a snake and were paid either a lot or a little money to be there. Those who received the smallest incentive suffered the most dissonance and changed their cognition about snakes. In other words, in order to make sense of why they spent time with a snake for such a small incentive, they had to decide that they were not that afraid of snakes to begin with.Subjects who received the large incentive should not experience cognitive dissonance since the incentive was sufficient to explain why they stayed in the room with the snake. Hence, their fear of snakes was not reduced.

In both of the above cases, clinical outcomes were obtained with only the use of social psychological forces.

## General Considerations

Regardless of the therapeutic orientation used, there seem to be some aspects of social psychological theory which play a role in successful treatment. As mentioned before, expectations in therapy are crucial. Sometimes merely making the commitment to go into therapy will produce some therapeutic gain. Waiting list control groups are frequently run in therapy outcome studies and have been known to be effective. Also, there seem to be some universal gains which can be related to setting fees and creating therapeutic gain through effort justification.

## CONCLUSION

This chapter has attempted to address the relationship between social psychological theory and clinical practice. As is obvious, there is much more theory than can be presented and many more therapeutic techniques than can be discussed. It does appear, however, that all therapies owe some of their effect to phenomena explainable through social psychology theory. Knowledge of this theory will make the task of being an individual therapist easier or at least richer. Any human interaction between two or more people (or often the expectation of that future interaction) is understandable in social psychological terms; psychotherapy is no exception. In the case of the individual therapy, almost every session involves some social intercourse and can, therefore, be better understood with some theoretical insight. In the final analysis, an awareness of the social psychological dynamics of the therapy situation may give the clinician an added sensitivity and understanding of psychotherapy.

## SELECTED READINGS

Bandler, Richard, and Grinder, John. *The Structure of Magic.* Palo Alto: Science and Behavior Books, 1975.

Corsini, Raymond (ed.). *Current Psychotherapies*. Itasca, Ill.: F. E. Peacock Publishers, 1973.

Goldfried, Marvin, and Davison, Gerald. *Clinical Behavior Therapy*. New York: Holt, Rinehart & Winston, 1976.

Meichenbaum, Donald. *Cognitive-Behavior Modification*. New York: Plenum Press, 1977.

Mikulas, William. *Behavior Modification: An Overview*. New York: Harper & Row, Publishers, 1972.

Morse, Stephen, and Watson, Robert, Jr. *Psychotherapies*. New York: Holt, Rinehart & Winston, 1977.

Rogers, Carl. *Client-Centered Therapy*. Boston: Houghton Mifflin, 1965.

Perls, Frederick S. *Gestalt Therapy Verbatim*. Lafayette, Calif.: Real People Press, 1969.

Chapter $3$

# Group Therapy

## CASE STUDY

Lisa glanced around the room at the strange faces. They were all so frightening to her. She had heard a lot about group therapy from her friends and had seen "sessions" on TV and in the movies, but at this moment her experience seemed so unreal. Five complete strangers, three men and two other women, sat silently staring at one another or looking at the floor waiting for Dr. Martin. When she finally did enter through the heavy oak door, there seemed to be a sense of relief in the room, but also a feeling of anxious anticipation.

"Good evening," she said. "I know this is the first time most of you have ever been in a group. Everyone (including me) will be a little nervous and distrustful in the beginning. What I would like to do tonight is just have us talk a little about ourselves and how we came to be here so that we can get to know one another a bit better. First, let's go around and say our names."

Lisa listened intently to the others as they stated their names. After everyone had introduced themselves, a long uncomfortable silence followed. Lisa thought of what else she might say but did not want to risk being the first to break the silence. The heavy silence continued. Lisa stared at her shoes, old friends by now, then she looked around the room. All of the other group members were looking at their shoes too, or so it seemed. She could feel the tension in the room. What could she say that would be important, but not boring to the others?

"I can guess from the silence that everyone is still a bit anxious about talking. That is perfectly natural, but we need to start somewhere." Dr. Martin looked carefully around the room. "Jim, why don't you begin."

Jim flushed noticeably, then cleared his throat audibly. "Ahem." He fell silent, then sheepishly looked up. "This is quite difficult for me," he said. "I'm afraid that what I have to say would not be very interesting to all of you."

"That's funny," Lisa thought, "I was thinking the same thing."

"Well," Jim continued after another pause, "I am not really sure why I am here. I guess that I am just not very happy. I have had the same job for ten years and I used to love it. Now I find it boring and I hate the people there. My marriage has also gotten sort of boring. I know that my wife is not happy, but I am not happy either. I supposed you could say that I am bored and confused."

There was a very long pause. After what seemed like ten minutes but was probably about two, Dr. Martin looked around the room and said, "Is there anything that any of you would like to say to Jim or share with him?"

Bob spoke. "I can really relate to what you are saying about your job. For a long time I wanted to be a lawyer more than anything in the world. Now I am a lawyer and I find that it's not all that I had it cracked up to be. But I get kind of a sick feeling in my stomach if I think about going into some other kind of work. I am not sure I can justify all that time in school if I change, but I really am miserable where I am now."

Other members of the group slowly began to chime in after Jim, speaking in vague terms about how they had been feeling badly recently. Lisa was continually amazed that people who looked to be much different than she in appearance, age, and manner all spoke of their problems in a way she could understand. One woman, Jackie, began to cry as she related the events that led up to the separation from her husband. Lisa felt that she herself might cry and actually reached over to Jackie, sitting next to her, and touched her arm. It felt good to do that, a warm, caring feeling.

Finally, Lisa felt that she must talk. Everyone had revealed a little about themselves and now she felt all eyes were on her. She did not want to be the only person who did not speak about her problem. She thought she might lose face with others. With that in mind, she managed to get herself to speak. She began by speaking of her "depression." She did not know why she was depressed, but speaking of it did make her feel a bit better. At first, she was afraid that others might make a joke at her expense, or worse, not even care what she had to say. Maybe they would not think her problems were as serious or as important as their own, or maybe they would think she was really sick. When she finished, she hesitatingly looked up at the others not knowing what to expect. But the others seemed sympathetic and did not laugh at her. A few asked questions which led Lisa to feel that they were interested in her and what she had said.

While the others had been speaking, Lisa noticed how much they tried to talk about their "feelings." She got the idea that she also should try to state her problem in terms of her feelings. "I often feel," she said, "as though there was a large brick in my stomach and a gray fog in my head." This had been going on for a number of years for her, since she left college and took a job teaching high school. At first it seemed like nothing too important, but after a year she was feeling no better and she was beginning to think that she might spend the rest of her life feeling this way. That really frightened her. Perhaps, if things did not get any better, life would not be worth living at all. That thought got her even more depressed; she had difficulty doing her work, keeping her apartment clean, and she even stopped going out with men or seeing any of her old friends from school. She was isolated and alone. Finally, one of her best friends expressed some concern and recommended that Lisa seek help. Now she was sitting here in the group wondering if there really was any help for her, feeling that her life has pretty much been a failure. She was stirred from her train of thought by the therapist's voice.

"Lisa," Dr. Martin's voice was soft and kind, "I appreciate your sharing your feelings with us. Many of us in here may feel like you, a bit confused about what is going on now for us. Hopefully, this group will help us to share with one another how we feel about life, our problems, and each other. When we can trust and feel good about the others here, we can hear them and help them and we in turn can be helped."

"I'm glad you said that, Dr. Martin." Frank, a man sitting across from Lisa spoke. "I would like to share a feeling with Lisa."

Lisa's heart began to pound.

"Lisa, I have been sitting here for a while now, wondering how it is that such an attractive person as you, so bright and. . . .and I don't know, so bright and beautiful, could possibly not feel better than you do. I know that I have problems, but you look like you are so depressed, I feel like I want to reach out to you, but you might reject me because you are so attractive."

It had been a long time since Lisa had thought of herself as attractive. She looked around the room at the other women and saw that she might be one of the most attractive people there. Her face began to flush and she was not sure how to respond to Frank. "I'm really not that attractive," she said. "If you knew me well you would know that I have a whole bunch of problems."

"Lisa, can you hear what Frank has told you without denying it?" asked Dr. Martin.

Lisa thought for a moment. She had not really believed what Frank had said. "Frank, I appreciate your feedback, but I am not really sure that I can believe it. I am really not that attractive or as on top of things as you might guess."

"You just did it again." Jackie spoke directly to Lisa. "You are denying what Frank said. Can you just hear it?"

"Thank you, Frank," Lisa said sheepishly.

During the rest of the first group session Lisa and the others spoke about how they felt about themselves and shared their perceptions of others. Dr. Martin tried to keep the group on task, and to ensure that everyone spoke a bit and was heard a little. She continually asked the group members to share their opinions with one another.

At the end of an hour and a half the first group was over. It would be getting together every week at the same time with the same people. Lisa was feeling a little better. She felt she had made contact with a few people and was looking forward to getting to know some of them better, looking forward but still afraid. She was still not sure exactly how the group was going to help her, but she did want to come again.

Over the weeks the group members became much closer as they shared things about their life—some important and some trivial. Lisa began to find out that others seemed to like her much more than she liked herself. They helped her to see herself in a better light and to accept both her strengths as well as her weaknesses. After six months, Lisa was feeling much better. She enjoyed the group and looked forward to it every week. She felt very close to Dr. Martin and the other members and felt that she could talk about almost anything to them. Shortly after that, Lisa felt good enough to leave the group. She had difficulty leaving her friends there, but she was no longer depressed. She did, however, keep in touch with some of the group members, but also found it seemed much easier for her to make new friends outside the group.

## SOCIAL DYNAMICS OF GROUP THERAPY

Human beings spend much of their lives in groups; they are born into a group (the family), educated in a group, and even buried with a group present. A number of theories in social psychology are aimed at explaining the dynamics of groups. These theories and the associated research offer some insight into the dynamics of group therapy.

Group psychotherapy is a rather recent phenomenon. The traditional model of therapy followed closely the medical model; the "sick" patient was healed by the doctor in the privacy of the doctor's office. The general view was that the client's problems were a matter of confidence between the therapist and the client. However, by the late 1940s psychologists realized that many of the problems individuals experienced involved interacting with groups of people. Hence, the best place to seek a "cure" for the problem was in the very environment in which the problem was experienced, i.e., the group. Thus, the last few decades have witnessed an explosive expansion of group therapy techniques.

The opening example typifies the type of interaction that takes place in many therapy groups. As we read the example, we can see Lisa's behavior changing over time. What caused these changes? What factors in the group setting influenced Lisa's behavior? It is to these and similar questions that we turn our attention.

*Conformity.* In the first session we can see that Lisa was very reluctant to speak out in the group. She felt nervous; she felt that she had nothing important to contribute; early in the session, she made up her mind not to speak at all during the first session. However, as the session progressed, we find that Lisa was feeling a great deal of pressure to "say something." No one explicitly told her to talk, but Lisa reports feeling this growing pressure as each of the other people talked. She finally succumbed and began talking about herself and her feelings.

In Lisa's case, the pressure to act as the other group members was helpful; it forced Lisa to get involved in the group, and to "open up." She expressed some of the things that were bothering her and finally allowed the group to help her cope with these problems. While conformity had a positive outcome in this case, we can think of numerous situations in which it does not. For example, one of the leading reasons teenagers give for smoking is that their friends are doing it. Many drug addicts say that they got started on drugs because their friends were using drugs.

Given that conformity can have such varied effects, why is it such a common behavior? Social psychologists have identified two ways in which the group pressures the individual to conform. The first is labeled **informational group pressure**. As children grow up, they learn that they often must rely on others to supply them with information. A child's parents may tell him to avoid wasps because they will hurt him. After catching one of the forbidden creatures in his hands, the child painfully learns that his parents were indeed correct. The next time his parents tell him to avoid something, he is more likely to respect their warning. Thus, the parents are able to influence the child because he believes that they are supplying him with correct information. Later, the child learns that other groups of people also are able to supply correct information. In some cases this information deals with the "proper" way to behave in certain situations. Because the individual believes that the group has the "correct" information, the group achieves the ability to influence that individual's behavior.

It is very likely that Lisa was influenced by informational pressure from the group. She was in a strange situation. She did not know what to expect or how to act, what was proper, what the psychologist wanted her to do. There was nothing in the situation that explicitly told her "what to do." The psychologist did not give her instructions about what to do. Thus, she looked to the other people in the group to see what they were doing. On the first day she heard Jim tell about how badly he had been feeling. She heard Jackie speak of the pain and depression surrounding her separation. Others also discussed their problems and the bad feelings associated with them. Lisa could see that the "appropriate" behavior in the group was to focus on one's immediate problems and, accordingly, Lisa's first statements involved her depression. In this case the information supplied by the group strongly affected Lisa's behavior. Had members of the group opened the session by talking about their childhood experiences, it is likely that this information would have influenced Lisa to also begin by talking about her childhood. Hence, the therapy group serves as a source of information and this information influences the behavior of group members.

Conformity is achieved not only through the group supplying individuals with new information about the appropriate way to behave. Deutsch and Gerard (1955) state that groups often exert **normative social pressure** to gain compliance from members. The basis for normative pressure comes from the individual's fear that he or she may be rejected by the group if group norms are not followed. Schacter (1951) and Freedman and Doob (1968) have shown that this fear is not unfounded; individuals who deviate from group norms are often ridiculed and rejected by the group. Thus, members may conform because they do not want to be rejected.

Normative social pressure also affected Lisa's behavior in the group. She had seen the group laugh at Frank when he suggested that the therapy session be opened by people telling about their educational and work background. She had seen Frank's hurt feelings following this rebuke. Even though she had not felt that Frank's suggestion was that unreasonable, she did not want to be the focus of group displeasure. Thus, rather than support Frank, she followed the majority example and began discussing her present state of depression.

Just as in the present example, conformity usually results from a combination of informational and normative pressure. Factors in the situation determine the extent to which each type of pressure influences the individual's behavior. For example, the less familiarity and experience an individual has in a particular situation, the more likely he will be influenced by informational pressure. Further, the more ambiguous the task or situation, the more likely it is that informational influence will affect group member's behaviors.

The distinction between informational and normative group pressures is of more than simple theoretical importance. Allen (1965) pointed out that an individual reacting to normative social pressure does so out of fear and anxiety. In such a case the individual may exhibit overt compliance without covert acceptance. That is, the individual may show behavior change only in the presence of the group. Once away from the watchful eyes of the group members, that individual is likely to resort back to old behaviors. This results because the individual was conforming only to gain group acceptance and not because he or she believed the behavior was correct. When the individual is removed from the group, there is no need to worry about group acceptance. On the other hand, conformity based on informational pressure is often accompanied by private acceptance in addition to overt compliance. In such a case, the individual assimilates the information because he or she believes it is correct. Thus, behavior change based on informational pressure is likely to endure when the individual is no longer in the presence of the group.

Looking at the example, we can note that Dr. Martin worked to see that behavior change in the group resulted from informational pressure rather than simple normative pressure. In the second session, the group members decided that one cause of Lisa's problems was that she did not express her anger. The group decided that when Lisa was angry, she should yell and shout. They attempted to force her to do this. At this point Dr. Martin injected that there are many ways to express anger and that while expression is desirable, it may be unwise to dictate how a person should express anger. At this point, the group members stopped telling Lisa how she should express her anger; they suggested that she may be more interpersonally effective if she allowed people to see clearly when she was angry. Lisa worked on this and by the end of the group she was much more expressive. Her expressiveness continued long after she had left the therapy group. Had Dr. Martin allowed the group members to utilize normative pressure, it is possible that Lisa may have yelled and shouted while in the group, but it is unlikely that she would have continued in this pattern when away from the group.

Conformity is clearly evident in almost every group

therapy session. Social psychologists have conducted numerous studies to identify the factors that determine the amount of conformity in a group. Studies focusing on individual characteristics suggest that the individual most likely to conform to group pressure may be characterized as one who (1) is attracted to the group, (2) expects to have future interaction with the group, (3) feels relatively incompetent in the present situation, and (4) does not feel completely accepted by the group (e.g., Dittes and Kelley, 1956; Raven, 1959; Worchel and Cooper, 1976). Asch (1951) found that conformity increased as the group size increased up to four persons. Then the amount of conformity leveled off so that conformity was about the same in a fifteen-person group as it was in a five-person group, Finally, conformity is greater when the group is faced with an ambiguous as opposed to an easy or clear task.

It is interesting to note that the above conditions are often characteristic of a therapy group. For example, Lisa was attracted to her therapy group but did not feel completely accepted by the group in the early stages. She expected to interact with the group over a series of sessions. She was unsure of the task that faced the group or how to tackle the problem. Finally, her particular group consisted of five persons—a size most likely to optimize conformity.

*Contagion.*    In the second session, Jim told of the tragic death of his twin brother and of the difficulty he had in coping with the loss. Lisa was moved by the story and wanted to hug and comfort Jim. She was reluctant to do so and held back. Jackie, however, was not and she moved next to Jim and put her arm around his shoulders. This action seemed to remove Lisa's hesitancy and she hugged Jim and cried for him.

At first glance, this action may appear to be an example of conformity: Lisa's behavior was similar to Jackie's. However, there was an important difference between this example and examples of conformity. Conformity involves a situation where the group creates conflict for the individual by pressuring him to act in a manner that was not his normal way. In the above example, the action of one of the group members reduced rather than increased Lisa's conflict; Jackie's behavior reduced Lisa's restraints about hugging Jim. This is an example of **contagion** rather than conformity.

Contagion is a common behavior in groups. You may have been in a situation where a crowd was gathered in a room with a No Smoking sign. A number of the people wanted to smoke but were reluctant to do so because of the sign. Finally, one individual lighted a cigarette and this seemed to trigger a number of other persons to start smoking.

The possibility of contagion is one of the distinct advantages of group therapy. Oftentimes individuals enter therapy because they have become locked into a non-functional behavior pattern. They may have ideas of other behaviors that they would like to utilize to cope with their problems but they are reluctant to try out these new behaviors. In the group therapy session, they see others performing in a way they have desired. This reduces their restraints against doing so and new behaviors are experimented with.

*Modeling.*     As the sessions progressed, Lisa paid closer attention to Dr. Martin. She admired the straightforward way Dr. Martin behaved. Dr. Martin was not afraid to express her feelings; when she was angry she said so and when she liked someone she came right out and said it. Lisa noticed the way Dr. Martin looked people right in the eye when she was speaking to them. Lisa also saw that the other members of the group responded very positively to Dr. Martin; they followed her suggestions, laughed at her jokes, and paid close attention when she spoke. In all, Lisa thought Dr. Martin was "pretty neat."

It was not until one of the later sessions that Lisa realized how close attention she had been paying to Dr. Martin. After the session, Jackie mentioned to her: "Are you thinking of becoming a psychologist? You're acting more and more like Dr. Martin everyday." Jackie smiled and added "But I like it a lot." This incident brought Lisa up short. She had indeed picked up many of Dr. Martin's mannerisms. She spoke out more straightforwardly, she held eye contact when she spoke, she even found that she nodded her head when listening to others speak just as Dr. Martin did. Lisa's behavior was indeed being affected by her imitation of Dr. Martin

Bandura and Walters (1963) suggested that one of the major mechanisms by which we learn new behaviors is through **imitation**. The other is by being reinforced for actions. The learning of new behavior through imitation particularly captivated Bandura and Walters' attention. At the time they were developing their social learning theory the controversy involving the effect of television violence on children was beginning to ferment. Two positions were developed. The first, based on the notion of catharsis, held that the watching of television violence allows the viewer to vicariously experience aggression. This would in turn reduce the individual's drive to aggress (e.g., Feshbach, 1961). The implication of this position was that we should not be too concerned about the violence children see on television.

The other position in this argument was exemplified by Bandura and Walters. They stated that viewing violence on television would lead to increased violence because the viewer would imitate the televised models. Further, the viewer would believe that that violence was a "good" behavior because he witnessed the model being rewarded for acting violently. In an effort to demonstrate this position, Bandura, Ross, and Ross (1961; 1963a; 1963b) conducted a series of studies in which children watched a videotape of a model beating a Bobo doll. The model punched the doll, kicked it, hit it with a mallet, and sat on it. Following this, the children were mildly frustrated and placed in a room with a Bobo doll and their behavior was observed. The results indicated that the children did indeed imitate the model's behavior; they hit the doll with the mallet, kicked it, and sat on it. Further results indicated that the children were more likely to imitate the model who had been reinforced for aggressive behavior than one who had been punished for it.

These studies demonstrated rather conclusively that learning does take place through modeling. We need only think back a decade or so for a clear demonstration that modeling also occurs among adults. In 1966, one of the first highly publicized airplane hijackings occurred. Before this airplane hijackings were rather rare. However, this early hijacking was vividly described in news reports. Soon after a number of airplane hijackings followed. They became so common that airports around the world were forced to spend millions of dollars installing antihijacking devices.

Turning back to group therapy sessions like the one described in the example, it is easy to see how members of the group may serve as models for one another. One individual may see another act in a manner that is rewarded by other group members. That individual may then imitate that behavior and if similar rewards follow, it is likely that the individual will continue to utilize that behavior. Because the therapist holds the highest status in the group and is often attended to (rewarded) by the group, he or she is most likely to become the model. This is one of the many ways in which the therapist may influence the behavior of group members without explicitly telling them how they should behave.

*Social facilitation.* In 1898, Triplett studied the times clocked by racing cyclists. There were a number of ways that the races were conducted. One was for the cyclist to race alone around the track to see how fast a time he could make. Another involved head-to-head competition where a number of cyclists raced at the same time trying to beat each other. Triplett found that the racers turned in much faster times when they raced in direct competition as opposed to racing alone against the clock. Almost forty years later Chen (1937) made careful observations of ants excavating tunnels. He counted the balls of dirt the individual ant removed from the tunnel. In some cases he had the ants work alone and in other cases he placed two or three other ants together. He found that the ant worked much harder (excavated more dirt) when in the presence of other ants than when alone.

Numerous studies aimed at investigating the effects of group presence on the individual's behavior followed these early observations. Robert Zajonc (1965; 1972) reviewed the results of these studies and concluded that the presence of a group tended to arouse the individual. This arousal facilitated or made more pronounced the dominant responses of that individual. For example, take the case of an individual who had learned well how to do a particular dive. According to Zajonc this well-learned behavior could be considered a dominant response of that individual. Hence, the individual should perform that response with more precision in front of a group than when alone. In Zajonc's terms, the group would facilitate the performance of that behavior.

This social facilitation effect has been found in a wide range of situations and across a number of types of behaviors. While there is still some controversy as to why the effect occurs (Cottrell, 1968), the results of the research indicate that groups facilitate the performance of dominant or well-learned responses and inhibit the learning or performance of new or nondominant behaviors.

These findings have important implications for group therapy. Looking at the opening example, we find that Lisa had been a shy individual before entering therapy. In the first session of therapy, Lisa was surprised to see how she acted. She knew she was anxious but even she did not expect her extreme shyness. In terms of social facilitation theory, we may describe shyness as one of Lisa's dominant behaviors. The group facilitated this behavior and caused it to be exaggerated. Bob, on the other hand, was a talkative, assertive person outside the group. In the group, this behavior was so evident that some of the group members resented Bob's brashness. When Bob was confronted with this, he responded that "He was not really like this outside the group." There may have been some truth to Bob's statement as it is likely that the group accentuated Bob's dominant response (assertiveness).

Social facilitation theory may also explain why group members often find it difficult to learn new behaviors in the group. For example, Lisa struggled with trying to be more assertive. She kept telling herself that acting assertive should not be that hard to do. However, she found that even the act of telling people when she was angry took a great deal of effort and concentration. This difficulty could be anticipated by social facilitation theory. As pointed out, the theory hypothesized that the presence of a group should inhibit the performance and learning of new or nondominant responses. In Lisa's case, expressiveness was a nondominant response.

*Risky shift.* One point is very evident in the behavior of the members of Dr. Martin's group therapy session; the individuals acted in a more "risky" fashion than they would have outside the group. In the first session, Frank openly told Lisa that she was "bright and beautiful." He told her that he was very attracted to her in the short time they had been in the group. This opennesss was a risk for Frank since he left himself very vulnerable to be hurt by Lisa. In the next session, Jackie hugged John and comforted him in a loving way. Again this was a "risky" action since John may have rebuked or rejected Jackie for this action. Jackie even commented on this when she said she had feared John's response but felt that she was willing to run the risk of being rejected. Jackie also made the interesting statement that she didn't think she could have done it if the group had not been present.

When we look at therapy groups we often find that individuals are more willing to take risks than they would be alone. This riskiness may involve disclosing intimate pieces of information or engaging in intimate nonverbal behavior. Interestingly enough, the role of self-disclosure is often greater in groups that in individual therapy sessions. What is it about a group that can account for this behavior?

One possible contributing factor was uncovered by Stoner (1961) while working on his dissertation at M.I.T. Stoner expected to demonstrate that being in a group tended to make individuals more conservative and cautious. He first asked individuals to respond to a series of choice dilemmas. For example, one dilemma described a prisoner in a Nazi POW camp. There was an opportunity for the POW to escape by hiding in a garbage can. A series of probabilities that the escape would be successful were then listed (1 in 10, 3 in 10, etc.). The subject was asked to indicate the lowest probability that would be acceptable for the POW to attempt the escape. After subjects had answered the questions alone, they were placed in groups of six to discuss the dilemmas and arrive at a group recommendation. When Stoner compared the average individual recommendation to that of the group, he found, to his surprise, that the group was actually riskier than the individual.

This experiment was followed by numerous others (e.g., Wallach, Kogan, and Bem, 1962; Burnstein and Vinoker, 1973; Blaskovich, Ginsburg, and Howe, 1975). In general, the studies supported Stoner's finding that groups make riskier decisions than the average individual. Further, the studies found that individuals themselves tended to become more risky after being in the group. One of the main explanations offered for this "risky shift" is that people value risky behavior in our society. Each person likes to think of himself or herself as being willing to take a chance. In the group individuals are able to determine the level of risk others are willing to take. Not wishing to appear unrisky or "square" the individual adjusts his or her behavior to appear no less risky than the average of the group. Hence, there tends to be a shift toward risk in the group.

This finding is certainly pertinent to the therapy group. No group member wishes to appear "closed" or unwilling to take risks. Taking risks and "opening up" are clearly valued in the group. Thus, when an individual observes other members taking risks, he becomes motivated to at least match this risky behavior. This cycle results in a tendency toward escalating risk in the group.

*Deindividuation*    Another explanation for the greater risk taking in the group may be deindividuation. In 1903 the sociologist Le Bon observed that individuals often become "lost" in the crowd and perform acts they would not perform if alone. Zimbardo (1969) further developed this position by suggesting that individuals often lose their own identity in a group and become deindividuated. Being deindividuated, the individual becomes less concerned with social evaluation and becomes less inhibited. He is more willing to engage in socially taboo behaviors.

The majority of the theorizing and research on deindividuation has been focused on negative behaviors. Zimbardo offered deindividuation as an explanation for the often-observed visciousness of crowds. He discussed brutal lynch mobs in which otherwise "law-abiding citizens" beat, torture, and burn their victim with an animal ferocity. If the individuals were alone they would be mortified by this behavior and certainly would never engage in it. However, being submerged into the group reduces their concern with self-evaluation and reduces their inhibitions. Zimbardo demonstrated that deindividuated individuals were more likely to behave aggressively than more individuated ones. It should, however, be noted that not all socially sanctioned behavior is negative. There are sanctions about the open expression of many positive feelings or with being too physically expressive with emotions.

According to Zimbardo, there are a number of variables that lead to a state of deindividuation. Among these are anonymity, large group size, altered state of consciousness (drugs and alcohol), arousal, and novel or unstructured situation. Another factor is an altered temporal perspective; the individual views the situation as temporary and thus focuses on the present and loses concern for the future.

A number of these conditions may be present in a therapy group. Looking at the chapter opening, we can see that Lisa did not know anyone in the group nor would she see them outside the group. The group situation was certainly novel to her and she was aroused by a mixture of fear, apprehension, excitement, and confusion. Further, she knew that she would be meeting in the group for only three months. After that, she would probably never see any of the people in the group again. Thus, she need not be concerned about their evaluations of her in the future. All of these factors may have conspired to cause Lisa to feel somewhat deindividuated and reduce her inhibitions about performing socially sanctioned behaviors. In this case, however, the sanctioned behaviors were not negative. They include self-disclosure of intimate information and nonverbal expressions.

Interestingly, a similar situation sometimes occurs between strangers in transient meetings in such places as on a train or in a bar. The two individuals meet for the first time and are soon discussing the intimate details of their lives and problems. They express things that they have never told their closest friends or spouses. After their relatively short interaction, they part company never to see each other again. This *stranger passant* effect has many of the characteristics that lead to deindividuation; the individual's remain rather anonymous to each other, their situation is novel, and they have a very altered time perspective—the focus on the present with no concern for the future. Thus, just as these factors reduce the inhibitions of the passing strangers, so too do they reduce the inhibitions of members of the therapy group. In both cases the result may be a positive one—the individuals "open up" and become very expressive in a relatively short time.

## APPLICATIONS IN CLINICAL PRACTICE

More than in any other mode of therapy, it would seem obvious that social psychology theory would have application to group psychotherapy. As we have seen above, however, there are many types of social forces in groups.

Different forms of group therapy may encourage or facilitate a variety of these social forces for the accomplishment of specific therapeutic goals In this section we will review how some of these forces may be enhanced in different group therapy settings using a wide spectrum of clinical techniques and making a number of distinct assumptions about the therapy process.

Most group therapies as actually practiced are combinations of many techniques. For this reason, it is more difficult to speak about a pure form of group psychotherapy than it is about an individual therapy. In addition, all group therapies share the underlying assumption that there is something in the nature of the group process which can be of great help in the treatment of certain individuals. This section will examine some of the differences in techniques given the fact that there is a great deal of conceptual and practical overlap among schools of practice.

Many attempts have been made by clinicians to categorize the major factors responsible for the effectiveness of group therapy. Yalom (1975) in his major work on group therapy posits eleven "curative factors." He believes that change occurs through the interplay of a complex set of human experiences. These experiences are the curative factors and can be facilitated in the group setting. As might be imagined, many of the major curative factors are social psychological in nature. Let us examine these factors from the social psychological perspective.

Yalom's first factor is the **instillation of hope**. He speaks of the clearly positive effect of having group members share with one another their problems, but also for them to observe one another improve during therapy. In addition, some group members may currently have problems which others have overcome. This may serve to allow group members to hope for some improvement. In social psychological terms, this instillation of hope is altering expectations in the positive direction. This process as discussed in the previous chapter, is crucial to success in all therapies.

A second curative factor according to Yalom is **uni-**

**versality.** Most clients who embark upon therapy believe their problems and their inability to cope with them to be unique to themselves. It is often reassuring to hear that others may have similar problems and/or feel they are incapable of dealing with them. For the social psychologist, the concept of perceived similarity is important in understanding attraction as well as conformity. If others are seen as similar to us, we may be more likely to like them, trust them, *and* be influenced by them.

The **imparting of information** is another important experience for group members if they are to show therapeutic gain. For Yalom, group therapy serves to teach clients about mental health and mental illness, about group dynamics, and about psychic functioning. The desire to gain information from the group is related to the emergence of informational social pressure in that group. This social pressure may also lead to the development of respect for the opinions and experience of others. Respect may produce yet another of Yalom's curative factors: **altruism.** Group members develop a desire to help others in the group. There often is a feeling of friendship and camaraderie between group members, almost a family feeling. Indeed, Yalom also believes that there occurs a **corrective recapitulation of the family group** with the therapists as the parents and the members of the group as the children. Parents are there to help the children and the children help one another. Another factor which is part of this help is Yalom's concept of the **development of socializing techniques** in the group. The group begins to help prepare its members for their life on the outside, when they are no longer in the group. This may be accomplished by helping members to deal with difficult situations which they may face between group sessions with people outside the group.

All of the factors above serve to strengthen the forces in the group to conform to the social pressures in the group, to imitate and model the leaders of the group (often in this case seen as parents), and to be like the other members in order to obtain continuing social support (normative social influence). This **imitative** behavior of the group members is another one of Yalom's curative factors.

Finally, Yalom speaks of the importance of **interpersonal learning** in the group; that is, having what he calls a "corrective emotional experience" in the psychodynamic sense. The group members learn about how people relate together in the social system of their group, an analogue to the social system in the real world. They also may learn about some more **existential factors,** philosophies of life of others, or other strong feelings about living and coping. Again, these represent socializing forces in the group, the transmission of values, usually through pressures to conform.

**Group cohesiveness** is a major effect of the process of functioning in the group. It promotes trust and binds the group together against perceived threats to members from the outside. It allows for the expression of trust between members and a feeling of mutual support. It sets the stage in many ways for the development of the perception that the group together can do much more than any of its individual members. This is social facilitation which may provide the further support members need to make more risky or previously unconsidered decisions. Members grow from each others' strength by witnessing each others' emotional experiences, a curative factor Yalom identifies as **catharsis**. The group begins to generate its own unique experiences, a bond between its members. The more cohesive the group, as a result of this bond, the less members wish to appear to be betraying the group by holding discrepant values or opinions. In essence, as the group grows stronger, members feel strong and healthy in the context of the group. They begin to feel safe and validated, cared for and significant. Yet, the paradox seems to be that the more they feel accepted for their uniqueness in the group, the more they become devoted to the values and the norms of the group and the more they are pressured to act like other group members. Although this may sound detrimental to the welfare of the members, it is often exactly the social experience they were lacking in their lives. It may be a move toward the adjustment of the person by having any positive social or group experience, especially under the "safe" supervision of a trained therapist. This last point is quite important. Group therapy is not the same as all other group processes in that the leader is not a member of the group. He or she serves not only as the therapist to individuals in the group, but represents the values of adjustment preferred by the society as a whole, a socializing parent.

Yalom's curative factors serve as an acknowledgment of the force of the group process. Other factors exist in all likelihood, spawned by other therapeutic orientations. Some of the factors can and, indeed, should be promoted by the group therapist, while others develop as a matter of course in any therapy group. The major task of the therapist is harnessing the energy of these forces in the direction most beneficial to the group members.

### Behavioral Group Therapies

*Overview.* It is important at the outset to distinguish between behavioral therapies such as relaxation training and desensitization which can be used on or taught to people in a group and those therapies which include the interaction of group members with one another. The former is little more than individual therapy done simultaneously with a number of people, while the latter is more group therapy in the sense of the previous discussion.

Most behavioral group therapies utilize the group to achieve behavioral goals. Most common among these types of groups are assertiveness training groups, habit control groups (e.g., weight reduction groups, groups to stop smoking), and skills training groups (e.g., social skills groups, study habits groups, etc.). Usually the groups are very structured, using other members for social support or censure, as actors in role playing or behavior rehearsal scenes, or as resources in developing new behavioral strategies. For instance, if Lisa were in a group to deal with her shyness in social situations, other group members might support her for carrying out behavioral homework given to her (e.g., meet one new person every day) or threaten to censure or fine her for not doing her assignments. Group members might also role play strangers for her to meet on the outside in behavior rehearsals during the therapy sessions. They might also help her generate new strategies for meeting people that she might not have thought of on her own. The major thrust of behavioral groups is to produce a new behavioral response in the person which was not there before, a response which is more adjusted in the context of her life or her avowed goals.

*Social psycholgical factors.*   It is easy to observe in the above examples, evidence of modeling behaviors in these types of groups. The modeling will be effective or not depending upon the characteristics of the model. As we have seen, people perceived as being similar to oneself usually make effective models. Also modeling by esteemed group members, most frequently the therapist, will be effective in promoting the desired behaviors. Lisa might watch Jackie play a scene of Lisa meeting someone on the bus. If Lisa really sees Jackie as being similar to her, Jackie will serve as a better model than someone Lisa sees as unlike herself playing that part.

Social facilitation may also play a part in encouraging a person to perform appropriate behaviors. If the individual desires to change certain behaviors, the presence of others making similar attempts to change may produce a competitiveness which encourages additional behavior change. In addition, the role of pressures to conform within the group may facilitate behavior change. No one wants to be the person who did not do the homework assignment, or who does not take a risk when all of the others have. Normative social influence plays an important role in motivating new and sometimes risky behaviors. If Lisa did not want to change, the social pressure may encourage her to do so. Likewise, suggestions about new strategies or behaviors may serve to promote informational pressures in the group. Members, seen as experts, may exert great influence over others in the group. These social forces are reinforcers for the desired behavior. A behavior therapist will maximize these forces by using group members to influence one another whenever possible, either to facilitate dominant behaviors which are appropriate, using contagion to model appropriate responses, or to encourage conformity pressure to change responses.

## Dynamic or Analytic Group Therapies

*Overview.* Rather than create a here-and-now reinforcement for new behaviors, analytic group therapies often attempt to recreate the emotional experiences of the past. They are designed to recapitulate the family unit and the emotional situations which produced the current difficulties in the group member's everyday functioning. Group members are used to facilitate insight into the past as it is reflected in current behavior, not to suggest new behaviors in the present. Emphasis is placed on recreating an old situation, producing a catharsis with insight, and then providing support for the emerging changes in the present. Many of Yalom's curative factors are constructed out of this psychodynamic model of therapy. The group must establish itself as an emotional force for the member in order to facilitate the reexperiencing of old emotions. This is analagous to the transference in individual therapy. The emotional force develops as group members interact with one another and recognize in the members (consciously or unconsciously) characteristics of significant others in their past life, most importantly, family members.

*Social Psychological Factors.* The goal in analytic or dynamic therapy is not just a content change in behavior (i.e., not just to change one undesirable behavior pattern) but is related to the process of how that pattern was determined by psychic forces in the past. In order to succeed, that process must recreate in the group those original conditions which allowed for the old expression of the psychic forces. To do this, the group must have some strong powers over the individual. Social psychologically, this power is exerted through the force of group cohesion, the feeling of trust which develops between group members, the socializing techniques used by the therapist and the members, and the pressures to conform in the group. All of these are similar to forces in the family of the group member and may help facilitate the catharsis and reexperiencing of emotions. The role of the therapist is to promote the group forces by guiding interactions among group members. Unlike many behavioral groups, analytic groups are often unstructured in that they do not involve specific exercises and the therapist does not actively lead the group. The therapist serves to help the important dynamics of cohesion and the other curative factors emerge by allowing interactions among members and attempting to facilitate the building of what Yalom (1975) refers to as the "group culture." The group culture is the unique feeling of that particular group as it develops the curative factors. In the case study, for instance, Dr. Martin tries to help build the group culture by asking group members to comment upon what others have said. She tries to steer group members passively into interaction with one another. The therapist attempts to allow for the projection of feelings not only on her, but upon other members of the group. The more people there are in the group, the more objects for transference and emotional discharge.

### Gestalt Group Therapy

*Overview.*    As with other Gestalt therapies, the emphasis is placed upon experience in the here and now. Many of the techniques used individually in Gestalt therapy are used in the group therapy setting. Group members are encouraged to share what they are experiencing related to others in the group (e.g., "When you say that, I get a sinking feeling in the pit of my stomach.") Group members are used to help others get in touch with their own experience by commenting upon what they see in the person and how that makes them feel. Gestalt group leaders will often use specific exercises designed to get group members in touch with their feelings. This may be done with the use of directed fantasies, dream work, or structured interactions. Frequently the leader will work with only one member, using themselves and group members as "props" to help the client get in touch with his or her experience in the here and now.

Gestalt therapy frequently makes use of a number of nonverbal and "touching" techniques. It is felt that because many people use their language to distance themselves from their experience, techniques which do not allow for the use of language should produce more direct contact with experience. Group members will often help in keeping the rules for nonverbal behavior and by commenting on the nonverbal communications they are receiving.

*Social psychological factors.* Modeling again plays a very central part in the Gestalt group therapy. Rules for experiencing in the here-and-now are alien to most group members at the outset. The leader especially must live by the rules and model appropriate functioning to the others. In addition, it is a major tenet of Gestalt therapy that growth cannot occur without risk. The leader must then facilitate the taking of risks by members in the group. The risky shift, when it takes place, is of great therapeutic value. The group norm develops in the direction of more and more risk taking, facilitating the experiencing of more and more new feelings, providing more material for the therapeutic endeavor. It is up to the leader, however, to select techniques which will allow for risk taking and to have people share their positive feeling directly with those taking the most risks. The leader, for instance, may ask directly for members to take a risk going around the room and may praise those in the group who have. Another method would be to get the members in touch with how it feels to take a risk by imagining doing it and then reporting their feelings to the group. The therapist might also have a member express his or her worst fear about what is happening now in the group or express directly to each other person in the room how he or she feels about that person right now. As this risk-taking norm develops, normative social pressure will ensure that others in the group will begin to take more risks.

Contagion may also operate in this sort of risk-taking group. As members take risks and are rewarded with positive experiences and positive feedback from other members, those who were inclined to take risks will feel freer to do so. It is important that the therapist be in control of the consequences to the person who models the risk taking for the group so that a model for contagion will exist.

## Client-Centered Group Therapy

*Overview.*   The assumptions of client-centered individual therapy hold true equally for the practice of client-centered group therapies. Clients are encouraged to help one another overcome the obstacles to their own self-actualization. The therapist takes a basically supportive position toward each member of the group. Sharing is encouraged as a way of showing support for one another in the group. The topics and issues to be covered are determined by the group members themselves.

*Social psychological factors.*   The forces which are the strongest in a client-centered group may vary because of the nondirective nature of the therapy. Depending upon the composition of the group and the types of issues members wish to be dealing with, feelings of similarity and desires for acceptance and information will be different. Some of these groups may develop very strong bonds facilitated by the acceptance they feel from the therapists and others in the group. They may feel good about being accepted and not want to be rejected. This may lead to greater conformity pressure as members wish to continue to be accepted. In Lisa's case, she may begin to feel good about Jackie, Jim, Bob, and Frank and how they can accept her. She may then go along with them so as not to threaten her acceptance by them.

Conversely, members may feel so accepted as to be able to say whatever they want without fear of attack or criticism. It may depend upon who emerges as the major models in the group. Again, modeling and imitation are important. In client-centered therapy, however, the therapist may not play a directive enough role to be a problem-solving model, although he or she may be able to model acceptance, unconditional positive regard, and empathy.

## T-groups

*Overview.* Although not strictly a therapy modality in and of itself, T-groups and T-group therapy have contributed to the construction of many therapeutic techniques used in group therapy. It is important to note also that the T-group method was developed out of social psychology rather than out of the needs and experience of clinicians.

T- or "training" groups according to Gibb (1975) can be described and defined by a number of criteria. The T-group has a here-and-now orientation which stresses existential experiences of the group, not the individual members. Emphasis is placed upon the process of the group and not the content issues. Groups have low structure and are usually not planned in advance or actively directed. The major focus of the group is upon *the group itself*, the social reality rather than the individual reality of the group members. Interactions in these types of groups are primarily verbal and strive for competence in the group task rather than therapy for the group members. Finally, it is the internal dynamic of the group which is the ongoing subject of discussion and experience.

*Social psychological factors.*   The T-group reflects the exploration of social psychologists of the group process itself. As such, it contains elements of most of the concepts we have been dealing with in this chapter as regards the social psychological forces in groups. It represents an attempt at self-examination of the group process. How an individual T-group will function depends upon the style and personal qualities of the leader and the population of the group. Usually, heterogeneity is desired in such a group. Inputs from all parts of the social or organizational sphere are incorporated to produce the most complicated and interesting process for the purpose of group self-study. Such groups may in some cases be supportive and in others be extremely anxiety provoking. Leaders may opt for an active supportive role (as in the case in Bethel groups) or an aloof and observing role (more the case in Tavistock groups). Some of the dynamics revealed in such groups can be applied to therapy groups or organizational management. Self-examination of the group process often enhances the forces which are present. This may produce an extremely intense experience for the members as they learn of the enormity and strength of the group forces. In essence, group members learn about the social psychological theory of the groups they are in and begin to examine their effects. If Lisa's group were a T-group, for instance, members might confront her about not talking in the group, or when she begins to talk, they might analyze her behavior for her in terms of theory (e.g., "You know, Lisa, ever since Frank spoke to you like that you have started to talk in the group. It may be that you have used him as a model, saw him talking, and then decided it was safe for you to talk.") The entire thrust of the group is toward this sort of analysis of the process of the group rather than *what* people are saying to one another. The group members are "trained" by their experience in the group to do this. Applications to therapy have been mostly in the area of encounter groups, designed to promote the group forces and bring issues related to the individuals functioning in the group to as rapid a head as possible allowing for their confrontation and resolution.

## Encounter Groups

Encounter groups are a broad category of group treatments not always remedial in nature. Some groups are designed to educate basically normal people into new areas of awareness. Such groups as sensitivity groups and sensory awareness groups deal not so much in therapy as in enrichment of the average life. The premise of encounter is to confront as rapidly and straightforwardly as possible areas of difficulty or ignorance, whether that be in personal relationships, sensory experience, or consciousness of political or social issues. A number of techniques are used to facilitate the confrontation. These may include confronting leadership style, purposeful selection of antagonistic members, extremely rigid rule structures, and marathon sessions. This last technique is one used in many therapies and needs a bit of explication.

Marathons are designed to employ physical and psychological fatigue in combination with prolonged group influence to create weakness in the usual defense systems used to screen out and make sense of our regular experiences of the world. This weakness represents an altered state of consciousness where group and individual forces appear to be heightened. With this increase at all levels of input, the power of the social psychological forces is magnified, allowing for more rapid confrontation. Modeling, conformity, contagion, risk taking, and deindividuation may all be enhanced if the group members are subjected to group forces without relief for long periods of time. Encounter may serve to facilitate accomplishment of the group goal in many circumstances, but it likewise may be dangerous if not done under conditions of control by trained practitioners who can prepare the group members to return to the world outside when the confrontation has ended or is at least in recess.

## Personal Growth Groups

Personal growth groups such as Human Potential Seminars are designed to help normal individuals contact potentials for experience and creativity in their lives of which they were previously unaware. A marathon format is sometimes used, but in general group forces toward conformity are used to encourage group members to explore themselves and their relationships with others. Most such groups are very structured and rely heavily upon prepared exercises and materials. These sorts of groups are not, however, therapy groups or designed to deal with severely maladjusted people.

## CONCLUSION

Group psychotherapy has been shown to be an effective form of therapy for many people. Depending upon the type of problem and the type of group technique used, success may be moderate to great. As with individual therapies, certain types of groups may be more effective with certain sets of symptomatologies. Adjustment problems or situational difficulties are often best treated with an experimental or problem-solving therapy rather than an insight-oriented analytic therapy. For more severe or chronic difficulties, analytic or long-term treatment may be indicated. This may be in part due to the fact that many of the social aspects of the treatment may be distorted or less powerful to persons suffering from severe neurosis or personality disorders. Much of this is speculation as it depends upon what specifically is done in the particular therapy performed by a particular therapist.

In general, it appears that the social forces which exist in groups play an important role in the effectiveness of group psychotherapy.

## SUGGESTED READINGS

Benne, Kenneth D.; Bradford, Leland P.; Gibb, Jack R.; and Lippitt, Ronald O. (eds.). *The Laboratory Method of*

*Changing and Learning.* Palo Alto: Science and Behavior Books, 1975.

Golembiewski, Robert T., and Blumberg, Arthur (eds.). *Sensitivity Training and the Laboratory Approach.* Itasca Ill.: F.E. Peacock Publishers, 1970.

Lieberman, Morton, A.; Yalom, Irvin D.; and Miles, Matthew B. *Encounter Groups: First Facts.* New York: Basic Books, 1973.

Sager, Clifford J., and Kaplan, Helen Singer. (eds.). *Progress in Group and Family Therapy.* New York: Brunner/Mazel, 1972.

Yalom, Irvin D. *The Theory and Practice of Group Psychotherapy,* 2nd ed. New York: Basic Books, 1975.

# Chapter 4

# Couples Counseling

## CASE STUDY

"Perhaps you could tell me a bit about why you have come to see me?" Dr. Evans folded his arms, took a deep breath, and settled back into his overstuffed chair. He looked alternately at the two young people seated on the couch as far apart as they could be. It was almost as though four other people had crowded onto the couch between them. They seemed to be physically repelled by each other like identical poles of two magnets. As the silence grew from seconds to a half minute, a small smile crossed Dr. Evans' face. Finally Dick Harris spoke as if from desperation.

"You are a marriage counselor, right?" His voice seemed hostile and a bit demanding.

"Yes, I am," admitted Dr. Evans.

"I guess we must need some counseling then, right?" Dick seemed very annoyed.

"That's what we are trying to find out," Dr. Evans spoke softly.

Another agonizing pause slipped by.

Finally, Betty spoke. "What my husband is trying to say is that our marriage is a mess and we desperately need help."

"Betty seems to think that since we argue sometimes that our marriage stinks and that it is all my fault."

"Dick, you know that's just not true." Betty began to squirm a bit in her seat. She crossed her legs and turned to face Dr. Evans. "He thinks that everything is just fine even though we hardly speak to each other at home and he has been sleeping on the couch for the past two weeks."

"I don't see how an outsider can help us, Betty." Dick flashed a piercing glance across the span of empty couch in his wife's direction. "He's probably not even married. And besides, we should be able to solve our own problems. Let's get out of here."

"Perhaps you both could tell me a little about what you are not getting from your partner right now in your relationship?" Dr. Evans injected calmly. "I would like to hear from both of you in turn. Dick, maybe you could tell me first."

"Well, despite what Betty will tell you, I am trying very hard in our relationship. I don't think she really understands what is going on with me at all. All she wants to do is get her way all of the time. I don't ask for much, just a little attention now and then and some sexual satisfaction. I don't think that she knows how important it is for me to have a good sexual relationship with my wife. My parents always did and that is something that I learned from them. My mother was such a loving, giving person. She lived for my father and they had a very happy marriage."

"Excuse me, Dick," Dr. Evans interjected, "You have said a lot about what Betty doesn't do, but what specifically would you like for her to be doing that she is not?"

"Well, she gets very moody a lot of the time. I know that means she is dissatisfied with something about me, but I never know what."

"Betty, Dick says that you are moody sometimes. Do you know what he is talking about?"

"I am not really sure. I know that I do get depressed sometimes and don't feel like talking to anyone, but that usually doesn't have to do with Dick. Since we have been married my mother and father haven't been getting along very well and are thinking of splitting up. Some afternoons she calls me up and cries for hours on the phone. That usually upsets me and I get depressed. I suppose that sometimes Dick sees me when that is going on."

"Dick, did you know about Betty's parents?"

"No, that's all news to me. I wish Betty had said something to me about it."

"Why didn't you mention it to Dick, Betty?"

"Well, he has had a lot on his mind and I didn't want to upset him. Besides, we have only been married about a year and have our own problems. I did not want to involve him in my folks' troubles. It might make him think I came from a creepy family or something." Betty now had a sheepish grin on her face, almost ashamed.

"Dick, how does it make you feel to not have Betty share the reason for her depression with you?"

"It makes me feel crummy, like I am not important to her."

"Is that what you were trying to communicate to Dick, Betty?"

"No! I love Dick very much and did not want to hurt him." She moved a bit closer on the couch.

Dr. Evans uncrossed his legs and spoke slowly. "So it appears that you, Betty, wanted to protect Dick and so you didn't share something with him that was upsetting. Dick, however, saw your depressed behavior and *assumed* you were depressed about something he had done. Then Dick acted toward you as if you didn't understand him because your behavior toward him seemed so unfair. You seemed angry at him but he didn't feel like he had done anything to merit that."

Betty interrupted, "I also guess I didn't want Dick to know about my family because then he would always be throwing up in my face that his family was more happy than mine and that he would know more than me about how to make a good marriage. I think I can be a good wife to him. I didn't want to be put down all of the time because of what my parents did."

"I wouldn't put you down, Betty. When have I ever done that?"

"I'm just afraid that you would." Betty had her head down and was looking at Dick almost sideways.

Dick moved closer to Betty on the couch and took her

hand. "I love you a lot, honey, and want to share things with you. That means the bad and sad things too."

Dr. Evans continued for a number of sessions with Betty and Dick helping them to ask for what they wanted from each other, and more importantly making sure that each heard what the other was saying. He found they frequently assumed they understood what the other was thinking and acted in accordance with their hunches. Sometimes these hunches were correct, but often they were not. Dr. Evans worked with them to make sure they understood what had been said by the other person to them, and what the intention of the remark was. He also asked them to examine how they saw each other, how they knew when the other was mad or in a bad mood, how they felt when, after checking nonverbal communication, they found that sometimes they were telling each other one thing but acting in a way that was inconsistent with what they were saying. For instance, when Dick would go out to play cards with his friends on Thursday nights, Betty would kiss him on his way out and tell him to have a good time. But he noticed that she was usually in her most flimsy nightgown at the time. Dick was getting two messages at the same time: go and have a good time but stay and have a good time.

The counseling with Dick and Betty in the beginning dealt with their problems in communications. After a while they were able to be clear with each other about what they were saying and hearing. Then, with the help of Dr. Evans, they turned their attention to solving the problems between them. Many were solved because they never understood the other's position very well, but some remained difficult. They worked for a long time on how to compromise with each other in such a way that each did not feel like the other always got the better deal or had the upper hand.

Finally, the counseling turned to dealing with how they could make space for each other to be different and still love and care about the other person. They worked on acknowledging the other for things they had done and seeing their differences as strengths in their relationship rather than weaknesses. This acknowledgment meant that they did not have to be better than the other at everything. It was OK for Dick to be better at some things and Betty to be better at others.

Dr. Evans worked with the couple over a few months to teach them the skills they needed to communicate clearly and solve their own problems. He didn't solve the problems for them. After a while he noticed that they were solving problems in sessions with little help from him. At that point he was finished with his counseling.

## SOCIAL DYNAMICS OF COUPLES COUNSELING

As can be seen from the opening example, couples therapy involves much of the dynamics associated with individual therapy. The therapist must be aware of the pressures that brought the clients to seek therapy—helping the couple will be a difficult job if one or both of the clients feels forced into therapy. The expectations of the clients are also important. The therapist's job is greatly complicated if either of the clients does not expect to be helped by therapy. Trust is also an important issue. Not only must the therapist gain the trust of the two clients but he or she must also help the clients trust each other.

While individual and couple therapy have much in common, there is an important difference between the two. In individual therapy, the therapist must be concerned with the thoughts and feelings of the client and with the interaction between himself or herself and the client. In couple therapy, these same concerns remain but the therapist must also be very sensitive to the interplay between the two clients. How do they interact in the therapy sessions? What verbal *and* nonverbal messages are they communicating to each other? The astute therapist will study the clients' interaction in order to uncover clues about their underlying problems.

*Negotiations and threat*   Dr. Evans learned a great deal about Betty and Dick from their discussion about the decision to enter therapy. It was clear that Dick did not want to seek counseling. Even though he felt they had a problem, he did not want to go into therapy. Betty's response to this was to accuse Dick of not caring about the marriage. She further countered by telling Dick that if he did not go into therapy with her, she would not go on the camping vacation they had planned together. Dick grudgingly gave in and promised to see Dr. Evans. However, he made Betty promise that they would not discuss his recent sexual impotence. He threatened to walk out of the therapy session if this subject was broached. Thus, the Harrises had settled into a routine of handling conflicts by threatening each other. This pattern was clearly evident in their discussion of the factors that led them to seek therapy and it became increasingly evident in the early therapy sessions.

Social psychologists have concentrated a great deal of attention on the area of interpersonal conflict and conflict resolution. Two major types of interpersonal conflict have been identified. The first involves conflict of goals. This is labeled **competition** and involves a situation in which only one party may emerge victorious. It is extremely difficult to resolve such conflict since one party's gain is the other party's loss.

The second type of conflict involves a conflict of means. In this case we are dealing with a situation where both parties have similar goals but prefer different means to achieve those goals. Such was the case with the Harrises: Betty and Dick both wanted a happy marriage. However, Betty felt that therapy was the way to help achieve this state while Dick did not believe this. This type of conflict is more easily solved than the competitive conflict.

However, the research indicates that even conflict of means is not likely to be solved when the two parties resort to threats. Deutsch and Kraus (1960) devised an interesting demonstration of this point. They led two subjects to believe that they each were the operators of a trucking company (Acme and Bolt). The aim of each subject was to move her truck along a route to the final destination as quickly as possible. The player could make money if the truck reached the destination in a short time. As can be seen from Figure 1, each subject had two possible routes: a quick straight one or a long winding one. The one catch was that the straight route had a one-lane stretch over which only one truck at a time could pass. If the trucks met in the center of this lane, one would have to back up before the other one could proceed. Here was the point of conflict: the truck that backed up lost time and money. How would the players resolve this conflict and settle on a way to use this short route?

In the situation described above, the two players quickly worked out a plan for alternating use of the straight road. In the end, both players won. In an effort to study the effect of threat on conflict resolution, Deutsch and Kraus employed two additional conditions. In one, they gave one player the ability to use a threat by lowering a gate (Figure 2) and blocking the other player's travel along the straight

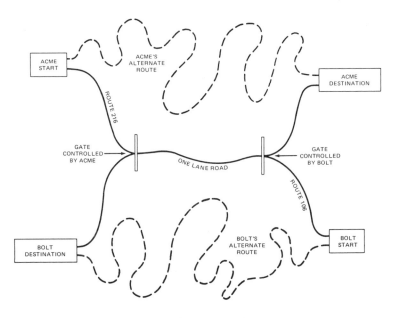

Fig. 1. Subject's road map

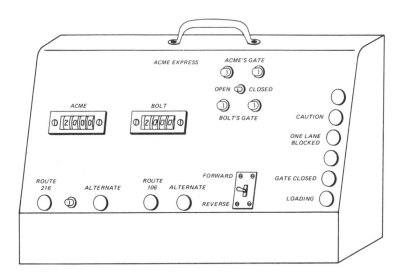

*Fig. 2. Subject's control panel*

route (unilateral threat). In another condition, both players were given the ability to threaten the other by lowering a gate (bilateral threat).

The results of these two conditions were startling. Neither player in either the unilateral or bilateral threat condition completed the course in time to win money. When players had the ability to threaten the other, they used their threat and this often led to a stalemate: neither player was willing to compromise after one had utilized threat.

Thus, the use of threat is very unlikely to lead to successful conflict resolution. One of the major reasons for this is that an individual who "gives in" to a threat may feel that he has "lost face." It may make one look weak to acquiesce to a threat. Goffman (1959) has agreed that there is a strong need in Western societies to maintain "face." It is very damaging to the individual's self-esteem to be publicly embarrassed or to lose face. Brown (1968) found that individuals often respond to a "face-losing" experience with aggression or threat. These are utilized to restore face. Thus, a threat by one party is likely to be met with a threat from the other party. This leads to a conflict-spiral (Deutsch, 1973) rather than to conflict reduction.

There is a second reason why threat is often met with counterthreat rather than compromise. Numerous studies (Solomon, 1960; Lave, 1965; Shure, Meeker, and Hansford, 1965) have found that a bargainer who is perceived as weak is often taken advantage of. For example, Solomon (1960) led subjects to believe that they were playing a bargaining game with an opponent. Unknown to the subjects, the opponent was programmed to be either unconditionally cooperative (give into the subject's demands on every trial) or to act in a tit-for-tat manner (when subject acted cooperatively, opponent acted cooperatively; when subject behaved competitively, opponent acted competitively). The results showed that subjects behaved more cooperatively with the tit-for-tat opponent than with the unconditionally cooperative opponent. Hence, it may be maladaptive to yield to threats and acquiesce. Such behavior may result in the individual's being taken advantage of.

Returning to the chapter opening example, we can see that Dr. Evans encouraged Betty and Dick to examine how they made decisions together. He pointed out his observation about the frequent use of threat and suggested that they discuss their feelings following decisions when threat was involved. He also pointed out his negative reactions to Dick's threat that "If I don't see some quick improvement in our marriage, I'm going to quit this therapy and handle things my way." These points seemed to help the Harrises a great deal as they worked to make decisions without resorting to threats.

*Psychological reactance.* Turning from the confrontive interactions of Betty and Dick, we see a very different style of behavior in Dr. Evans' interactions. Dr. Evans acted in a supportive fashion and often made interpretive statements. He was also very careful not to force either Dick or

Betty to discuss issues. He would make suggestions about topics for discussion but he never ordered Dick or Betty to talk. For example, in the first session Dr. Evans attempted to get the Harrises to focus on their own relationship by suggesting, "Perhaps we could begin to explore what you are not getting from your partner in your relationship. Dick, would you be willing to give me some of your thoughts on this issue?" In this case, Dr. Evans guided the direction of the discussion by involving the Harrises in the decision. He did not force them to take this position.

According to Jack Brehm's theory of psychological reactance (1967), this course of action should be very important in gaining the cooperation of the clients. Brehm states that each individual has a set of "free behaviors" that the individual feels he or she can engage in either at the moment or at some time in the future. In a therapy session, a client's free behaviors may include the freedom to determine what topics will be discussed with the therapist. According to Brehm, a threat to or elimination of a free behavior will psychologically arouse the individual and motivate him to restore the threatened or eliminated free behavior. This arousal is labeled **psychological reactance**.

Research has shown three types of reactions following the arousal of reactance. First, the individual may attempt to directly reestablish his freedom by performing the threatened free behavior. Hammock and Brehm (1966) told children that they could choose a candy bar as a reward for being in an experiment. The experimenter then attempted to influence their choice by telling them that they should not chose candy bar X. In essence, the experimenter threatened their freedom to chose candy bar X. The subjects responded to this threat by choosing candy bar X, thereby restoring their freedom to have this particular bar. A second response to threats to freedom is that the threatened free behavior increases in attractiveness. For example, if you felt that you should have the freedom to see a particular movie but found that the freedom was eliminated because the movie had been banned from your town, that movie should increase in attractiveness. Finally, aggression aimed at the threatening agent has been found to follow the arousal of reactance (Worchel, 1974).

Applying reactance to the therapy session, we can see that Dr. Evans' attempt to involve the Harrises in deciding the topic of the session was a prudent behavior. Presumably, Dick and Betty felt that one of their free behaviors was choosing what to discuss in therapy. Dr. Evans would have threatened this freedom if he had said, "Now, I want you to tell me what you are not getting from your partner." Such a comment would likely have aroused reactance in the Harrises. They may have met this statement with hostility and refused to talk on this issue. By involving Dick and Betty in the decision, Dr. Evans did not threaten their freedom. Hence, he enhanced the possibility of gaining cooperation from the Harrises.

*Coalition formation.*    A particularly tense moment during the first session involved the argument between Betty and Dick about who was to blame for Betty's failure to discuss her family's problem with Dick. Betty stated that it was Dick's fault because he never expressed interest in her family and he never seemed to have time to talk about problems. Dick, on the other hand, blamed Betty. "She is too timid. She never tried to talk to me about the problem. I feel that if it had really been important, she would have made sure I found out about it." The bickering escalated though neither party was having success convincing the other. Then an interesting series of events began to unfold. Dick turned to Dr. Evans and said, "You agree with me, don't you Dr. Evans? I'll bet if your wife has something important to say, she comes right out and says it." Dr. Evans responded to Dick by suggesting that it may be helpful to explore why Betty felt she couldn't discuss problems with Dick. Betty then quickly responded by saying, "See, Dick, he doesn't agree with you. I think Dr. Evans is right; we should look at what you do that keeps me from talking to you." She then added, "Thank you for pointing that out to Dick." Dr. Evans then corrected Betty: "I'm not saying that the fault lies with either Dick or you. I think you two have a problem in communicating to each other and rather than place blame, it should be more helpful to discuss how to resolve the problem."

This incident is interesting because it demonstrates how both Dick and Betty sought to enlist the aid of Dr. Evans on their side when conflict arose. Both seemed to have the idea that a coalition of two persons could "beat" a single opponent. Throughout the session, Dr. Evans encountered these coalition attempts. Oftentimes, they involved either Dick or Betty trying to force him to take their side. However, at times Dr. Evans found himself the "odd man out" as Dick and Betty teamed up to present a united front.

The question of when and how coalitions form has intrigued psychologists, sociologists, and political scientists for years. Individuals or groups often attempt to augment their power of recruiting allies. Theodore Caplow (1956) conducted the pioneering work on coalition formation in triads. Caplow felt that the type of coalition formed would depend on the power of the parties. When one party was more powerful than a combination of the other two parties, no coalition would be formed. This follows because the high power party will not be interested in a coalition because he has nothing to gain from it. Further, there is no reason for the low power parties to unite since their combination would not defeat the high power party. If we look at the beginning sessions in couple therapy, it is clear that the therapist is more powerful than the two clients. Thus, as in our example, Dick and Betty tried to elicit Dr. Evans' support but they rarely combined their efforts to attack Dr. Evans. Another of Caplow's predictions was that when one party was more powerful than either of the other two but not more powerful than a combination of the two weaker parties, the weaker parties would form a coalition. Returning to the therapy example, it is likely that as the clients began to feel more comfortable in the therapy situation, they also felt a gain in their own power relative to the therapist's. This becomes evident as they attempt to assume greater control of the session and play a more active role in determining the issues discussed. Another consequence of this augmentation in power is that the clients are more likely to form a coalition in later sessions. They still feel that the therapist has more power than either one of them but they may not feel that their combined resources are equal to the therapist's.

In our example, we see that as the sessions progressed, Betty and Dick came to each other's support more often. At times they even challenged Dr. Evans. This was a very important process in the therapy and Dr. Evans did not discourage it. One of the major problems that Betty and Dick had experienced was a lack of togetherness. They did not listen to each other's problems, they did not work together, and neither felt that they had the support of the other. This slowly changed in therapy as they found themselves coming together more often. When they formed coalitions, they supported each other and combined their efforts. They experienced the pleasant feeling of being together rather than on "opposite sides of the fence." This experience carried over and they began trying to better coordinate their efforts outside the therapy sessions.

*Self-other attribution.* An important issue in the first therapy session involved the "different way" Betty and Dick perceived each other. For example, they both agreed that Betty had been upset a lot lately but they disagreed about the cause. Dick's explanation was: "Betty cries a lot and acts depressed a lot. There isn't much I can do about it because Betty is just a moody person." Betty, on the other hand, responded: "I do cry a lot but it's not because I'm moody. I'm sensitive to the situation and I just get upset when there are real things to get upset about. I cry because my parents are having so much trouble. I get upset when we don't have enough money to pay all our bills."

In essence, Dick blames Betty's behaviors on her **dispositions**. Betty, on the other hand, blames her behavior on the **situation.** This is an interesting difference but Jones and Nisbett (1971) have argued that it is a common occurrence in attribution. They suggest that there is a pervasive tendency for actors to see their behavior as being caused by the situation while "observers tend to attribute the actions to stable dispositions" (p. 80). McArthur (1972) demonstrated this effect by asking volunteer subjects why they consented to be in a study. Their general response was that their participation was motivated by the importance of the study (situation). McArthur then gave observers written accounts of the request given to participants and their consenting statements. The observers were asked why they thought the participants agreed to be in the study. The observers tended to give dispositional reasons (the participants were friendly or altruistic people).

What can account for these differences in attribution? Jones and Nisbett offer two possible explanations. First, actors are aware of their past behavior while observers are not aware of how the actors responded in past situations. Hence, the actor may know that he is not always friendly, helpful, or moody. The observer oftentimes does not have this information. A second reason involves the focus of attention. When an actor behaves, his attention is focused on the situation; he often pays little attention to himself. On the other hand, the attention of the observer is usually focused on the actor. Hence, when each is asked the reason for the response, the attributions are based on the most salient information.

When the attributions involve negative behavior such as Betty's moodiness, a third reason can account for the actor-observer differences. We all wish to see ourselves in the best light possible. It is not very flattering to label ourselves as cruel, moody, or hostile. One way to preserve a positive self-image after we have acted in a negative manner is to attribute the cause of the behavior to the environment. Thus, we may say that I am a kind person who hit that small child because he was naughty.

Thus, the actor and observer may attribute different causes to the same behavior. As in the case of Betty and Dick, the actor and observer may be perplexed as to how such different causes may be attributed to the same behavior. One cause may not necessarily be more correct than the other. However, as Dr. Evans pointed out, "In order to better understand each other, it is important to see how two people may take different views of the same behavior."

*Nonverbal Behavior.* Dr. Evans not only listened to the words spoken by Betty and Dick, he also noted their behavior. In the first session, he noticed that Dick and Betty sat at opposite ends of the couch leaving as much space as possible between them. He saw that Dick leaned backwards and smiled a great deal when he boldly offered, "There's not really anything wrong with our marriage, I'm not worried at all. Everyone has their good days."

Social psychologists such as Birdwhistle (1952), Ekman (1968), and Mehrabian (1971) have pointed out that human beings communicate through two channels: one verbal and the other nonverbal. In our everyday conversations, we often fail to pay attention to the nonverbal messages. This is unfortunate because while individuals may speak untruth, as Ekman and Friesen (1969) point out, "nonverbal behavior may escape efforts to deceive, may evade self-censoring or may betray dissimulation." Since nonverbal behavior is often emitted unconsciously, it is difficult to lie through nonverbal channels. Further, Mehrabian (1971) found that nonverbal behavior may be observed to detect an individual who is lying verbally. Mehrabian found that when communicators were lying they exhibited less frequent body movements, tended to learn backwards, smiled more often, and placed more distance between themselves and the listener. Thus Dr. Evans was able to see that Dick was not feeling as confident about his marriage as he expressed in words.

In addition to "giving away" deceit, nonverbal behavior often expresses attraction. Attraction may be communicated nonverbally in a number of ways. For example, Hess (1965) reported that ancient Chinese jade dealers carefully watched the eyes of prospective buyers. The jade dealers felt that the buyer would spend longer looking at a piece of jade to which he was attracted and that the pupils of his eyes would dilate when he was interested in a piece of jade. Research (Argyle, 1967; Exline and Winters, 1965) has shown that individuals who like each other spend more time looking at each other than individuals who do not like each other. Hence, there is truth in the idea of the "lover's gaze."

Interpersonal distance can also communicate attraction. Lett, Clark, and Altman (1969) cited forty studies showing that individuals who like each other stand closer together when communicating than individuals who do not like each other. Along these same lines, Hall (1966) suggested that individuals have definite distances at which they are comfortable interacting. According to Hall, people feel a certain sense of ownership of the space immediately surrounding them. If someone intrudes into this personal space, the individual will move to restore his or her space. One of the main variables that determines how close one is allowed into this personal space is the relationship between the individual and the intruder. A friend is allowed to come closer than a stranger. Thus, as people become friendlier the interaction distance between them shrinks.

Dr. Evans observed the Harris' nonverbal interaction. In the early session Betty and Dick rarely looked directly at each other when talking. They also sat far apart during these sessions. Even though they said that they loved each other as much as the day they were married, their nonverbal behavior cast doubt on this. However, as the therapy progressed and the Harrises worked through many of their conflicts, Dr. Evans noted marked changes in their behavior. They talked to each other more and held eye contact when conversing. They sat closer together and touched each other more often. Interestingly enough, as their nonverbal behavior became more intimate they seemed less concerned with convincing Dr. Evans that they were happy together—their behavior spoke for itself.

*Summary.*   The interpersonal dynamics involved in couple therapy encompass many of those involved in individual therapy. However, in addition to the therapist-client relationship, attention must be focused on the client-client relationship. Oftentimes, partners in a relationship attempt to solve their conflicts by utilizing threats. Research on conflict resolution suggests that this is not an effective means. It is likely to lead to a stalemate as both parties work to save face and refuse concessions. Such threats may also arouse psychological reactance. In this case the threatened freedom becomes more attractive and the individual may perform the threatened behavior simply to restore his or her freedom. Coalition formation is also likely to result during couple therapy sessions. Each client may seek to gain a power advantage by forming an alliance with the therapist. A coalition between the two clients may also be formed in order to manipulate the therapist. Couples often find themselves at odds because they interpret each other's behavior in different ways. Social psychological research has found that actors often see their behavior as situationally determined while observers attribute the behavior as arising from the actor's stable dispositions. The addition of a third person to the therapy session increases the amount of nonverbal communication in the sessions. Because body language is emitted unconsciously, it is difficult to use this channel to communicate deceit. Interpersonal attraction is one of the major messages signaled nonverbally. Individuals who are attracted to each other spend greater time looking at each other and interact at closer distances than individuals not attracted to each other.

## APPLICATIONS IN CLINICAL PRACTICE

The field of marriage and couples counseling is relatively new in comparison to individual and group psychotherapy, and in some respects is quite different in terms of goals and methods. In the first place, couples work is directed primarily at the functioning of the relationship much more than the individual. Second, the two people engaged in that relationship selected each other. In other therapies the therapist selects the clients or the group members, often with an eye toward facilitating certain social and emotional forces to the benefit of the participants.

The goals of the couples or marriage counselor are not necessarily related to keeping the couple together, but rather to allowing them to more deeply and fully explore their relationship so that they can make an informed decision about reaffirming or resolving their commitment to one another.

All of the social psychological factors mentioned above play an important role in how counseling is to proceed. This work is often best accomplished through assessment of the situation using clinical sensitivities based upon careful questioning and observation, and then a counseling phase which must include at least six steps to neutralize the negative process in the relationship and allow for the rediscovery of any feelings that the couple may have for one another.

First, however, the task of the couples counselor (many of these people are therapists or psychotherapists, but work with couples is usually considered to be counseling rather than remedial therapy) is to determine the clients' commitment to each other and, therefore, their commitment to work in the counseling setting. Careful attention must be paid to both verbal and nonverbal cues exhibited by the counselees. Frequently, one of the members of the couple is interested in saving the relationship while the other is interested in having the counseling fail so that they cannot be seen as culpable in breaking up a relationship they would like to dissolve. This may produce an attempt to sabotage the therapy in and out of the counselor's office. This sabotage may be done overtly (e.g., Dick's argumentative style in the sessions) or covertly by missing sessions, forgetting the car keys, or just not responding in sessions. It is possible in many instances for the perceptive counselor to become aware of resistance by attending to the verbal and the nonverbal behavior of the clients. There will often exist a discrepancy between what is verbally stated and what is indicated nonverbally either to the counselor or the partner. This "incongruity" usually indicates that at some level there is some question about commitment either to counseling or to the relationship. The counselor must examine these discrepancies to determine if there is sufficient motivation on the part of both members of the couple for counseling to succeed. If there is indication that commitment is present, the counselor should endeavor to foster change by employing at least the following six steps, each one based upon a part of the social psychological theory presented earlier in this chapter. These steps have been formulated through examination of theory and the experience of therapists (Bach, 1968, 1970, 1974; Bandler, Grinder, and Satir, 1976; Koch-Sheras, 1978). They represent, we believe, some of the major issues which need to be addressed in order to effectively work with couples.

The first step the counselor must take is to prevent the formation of hostile coalitions (e.g., one of the couple and the counselor against the other). This will serve to reduce the perceived threat felt by each member of the couple. This threat may be in the form of a fear that the counselor may blame them for the failure of their relationship, or that their partner may blame them for the poor state of the relationship. The counselor must be firm and explicit in stating that he or she is not a judge or a referee, but a guide. Blame will not be the issue in the counseling, just the resolution of conflict. The counselor must then behave in a way that models this desire not to blame by not judging the members of the couple, and not being drawn by either person into a position to judge (e.g., Do you really think that is fair, Doctor?"). The counselor must protect the members of the couple when they are not being treated fairly and convey a sense that each of them is as good as the other and that both have tried hard in the past to make their relationship work. The question now is not "Whose fault is it that it failed?" but rather "What shall we do now?" It is often necessary for the counselor to explicitly set up rules for fair play and give homework assignments to allow for the fair play to be practiced. This will prevent the negative coalition from forming. Dick and Betty kept trying to draw Dr. Evans into a coalition by asking his opinion, or assuming that he was on their side. (e.g., Betty and Dick kept telling Dr. Evans what the other was saying, trying to exaggerate it so Dr. Evans would side with them).

The second step in treatment is for the counselor to facilitate clear communication between the partners (Bandler, Grinder, and Satir, 1976). Usually, part of the difficulty between the members of the couple is that they do not clearly understand the other person although they think they do. Sometimes, nonverbal messages and verbal ones are inconsistent and the person does not know which to believe. He or she may misinterpret statements and actions to mean what they were not intended to mean. Frequently intentions may be misattributed. The task of the counselor is to begin to understand how each of the members of the couple views the world and then to translate the communications for them into each other's communications system. It is not uncommon for two individuals in a couple to see things in entirely different ways. One person may be extremely cognitive and abstract while the other is more concrete or emotional. One member of the pair may use visual imagery to represent the world while the other uses feeling or kinesthetic images or auditory ones. This may produce a high level of frustration as the couple does not realize that each sees the world and communicates it differently. The frustration is increased when each person believes that he or she is trying hard to be communicative and can only attribute the lack of success to the partner's lack of caring or interest. It is up to the counselor to determine if there really is a lack of caring and to enable the two parties to communicate their intentions to one another. The primary task is for the counselor to be the translator (e.g., "When your husband says that you are not a good housekeeper, maybe he does not mean that you are a failure as a wife.") In this way the couple can be helped to at least begin to understand the communications of the other person. Then, the counselor must teach the couple how to clarify the communications for themselves. They must learn to ask each other to be more clear. This demand for clarity must be couched in nonthreatening terms by the counselor. ("Just because you are not being understood does not mean that you are not being clear or that the other person is stupid, it merely means that you are not communicating.") Teaching techniques to the couple which involve "echoing" what each has heard the other person say can be extremely helpful in teaching clear communication skills.

Once the counselor has accomplished the second step, the third phase is to clarify misattributions by using the clear communication skills which have been learned. This is done by asking the couple to be explicit about feeding back to the communicator what they hear, see nonverbally, and *assume* about what is being communicated. For instance, when Dick said that his wife was frequently moody, he *assumed* that meant she was dissatisfied with him. In this part of counseling he would be encouraged to check out with Betty if she is indeed dissatisfied with him and if that is the way she expresses her dissatisfaction. Chances are good that he has, in this case, misinterpreted her behavior. He will act on the basis of what he thinks she is doing and she will respond to that even though she may not be able to make sense of why he responded to her the way he did. This will promote further misattribution and more miscommunication. Once the misattributions are cleared up and the partners are no longer reading each other's minds, the real problems of the relationship may be addressed.

The fourth step for the counselor is to facilitate positive, supportive coalitions, first between each of the partners and himself or herself. This can be accomplished by attempting to understand and empathize with each person's frustration and difficulty. It is important that both parties feel that the counselor understands them. Then the counselor can proceed to promote a coalition between the partners against the common enemy, their problem. In this way the threat to each other will be minimized and this will facilitate further communication and solidify their responsibility and they cannot so readily blame the other. Once this skill has been acquired by the couple, they may use it to deal with long-standing obstacles to their good feelings about one another, past hurts.

A fifth step is to facilitate the exploration of "past hurts" by the couple. They must approach this not from blame, but from a desire to understand what is painful to the other person, and how it was that the hurts occurred. Oftentimes the most significant past hurt for one of the people was never even perceived or acknowledged by the other. It is important that events which have shaped the past of the relationship are revealed, not for the purpose of rectification, but in order to allow for dealing with hurts as they occur in the present. This step will, in effect, neutralize the weapons which threaten the other person and allow them to negotiate. No relationship is completely mutually satisfying to both people all of the time. What allows this type of partnership to succeed is an ability to cope with the hurts and problems as they arise, not to use them as weapons to threaten the other (e.g., you hurt me so now I can hurt you). Once this can be done, free expression of feelings can take place. When this is possible, the final step is taken.

The sixth step then is for the couple to reassess and renegotiate their relationship honestly without threat or blame. They should, by this time, be able to express their needs and feelings clearly to each other and negotiate for what they want from each other, or to see that it is not possible to continue the relationship. If they truly have developed an understanding of each other, the negotiation can be done without mutual threat. This will produce, as mentioned above, a more effective settlement even though the relationship as it was previously defined will no longer exist. The counselor must help in the negotiating by continually demanding clarity from the couple.

When all of the above steps have been accomplished, the major work of the counseling is finished. The major thrust of the entire endeavor is to produce the ability to negotiate truthfully and without threat to the other person.

## CONCLUSION

Couples counseling is based upon bargaining skills. In order to be successful, participants must be able to communicate clearly to avoid reactance, antagonistic coalition formation, threat, and misattribution. An effective counselor must be able to facilitate clear communication between the parties and create an atmosphere free from threat and blame.

## SELECTED READINGS

Bach, George R., and Deutsch, Ronald M. *Pairing.* New York: Avon Books, 1970.

Bach, George R., and Goldberg, Herb. *Creative Aggression.* New York: Avon Books, 1974

Bach, George R., and Wyden, Peter. *The Intimate Enemy.* New York: Avon Books, 1968.

Bandler, Richard; Grinder, John; and Satir, Virginia. *Changing With Families.* Palo Alto: Science and Behavior Books, 1976.

Sager, Clifford J. *Marriage Contracts and Couple Therapy.* New York: Brunner/Mazel, 1976.

# Chapter 5

# Family Therapy

## CASE STUDY

"I just don't understand. We have had a happy family all along until Tommy started acting up." Bob Davis was visibly exasperated. "You are supposed to be the family expert, Ms. Fargo, what do you think?"

"We have tried so hard to be good partners to both of the children," Bob glanced at his wife, "but Tommy just doesn't respond anymore. I wish he was more like his little sister. She is so well behaved and is a joy to have around."

Tommy sat motionless in a chair gazing out the window. He was fourteen and a bit small for his age. He looked completely disinterested in the proceedings.

Sissy was eleven. She was sitting on the couch between her Mom and Dad with a smile on her face. Across from them sat Ms. Fargo, the family therapist.

Ms. Fargo spoke. "Could you be a little more specific about the changes you have seen in Tommy and when they came about?"

Mrs. Davis answered first. "Well, I guess it was about two years ago. Tommy started getting in fights at school. When we talked to him at home he said it was none of our business. He became moody and disobedient. He wouldn't do anything that we wanted him to. He began to act mean to his sister and even hit her."

"What about the fights at school?" Ms. Fargo asked.

This time it was Mr. Davis who spoke first. "Ginny was

more worried about them than I was. I used to fight a lot when I was in school and I think it is normal. I had a lot of brothers and sisters in my family and I learned early that I had to fight for whatever I could; its part of being a boy. But I was very respectful to my parents, especially my Dad. If I ever got out of line he would smack me one."

"Have you ever had to hit Tommy?" Ms. Fargo inquired softly.

"Sure, a couple of times, but it didn't seem to do any good."

All at once Tommy seemed to be paying attention, his eyes riveted on his father. "Yeah, he hit me a lot, for no reason at all!"

"Now, that's not true, Thomas," Mrs. Davis has a scolding expression on her face. "If you behaved yourself a little better you wouldn't get hit. Ms. Fargo, I can't say that I am in favor of the hitting, but I understand sometimes how frustrating it may be for Bob."

"You don't know how frustrating it is for me, honey." Bob seemed upset. "You don't have to work all day at the office and then come home to contend with all of this. Sometimes I feel like I don't even want to come home."

Ginny gave him a hard stare. "You think things at home are easy all day? I could use some support from you. You think all you have to do is earn the money and I will do everything else. Well I am not about to do that anymore."

"As you can see, Ms. Fargo, Ginny and I do not see eye-to-eye on everything about raising the kids. I think she is afraid that she has failed Tommy in some way."

"I've failed?" Ginny's face was now getting red. "You are the one who is never around to provide a good example for the kids. They have a mother; what they need is a father."

"I think you can see, Ms. Fargo," (Bob winked at the therapist) "what I am up against here and why it is no fun to come home anymore."

There was a long tense silence.

"What about you, Sissy," Ms. Fargo looked at the little girl, "what do you think about what's happening at home?"

"I think Tommy is a bad boy. I wish he would stop hitting me. I liked him before when he was nice."

Tommy began to fidget and finally he got up from his chair and started to walk around the room.

"Sit down, son," Mr. Davis demanded in a firm voice. Tommy ignored him.

"Sit down before I knock you down!"

Tommy reluctantly sat down in a chair in the far corner of the room.

Mrs. Davis began to cry. "I just don't know what to do anymore. Things just seem so hopeless. Why can't people be nice in this family anymore? I don't think I am asking too much, am I?"

Ms. Fargo spoke thoughtfully. "I get the feeling that people in this family would like things to be different. Bob, I can see how frustrating it must be for you to work so hard and not be able to relax when you get home. And, Ginny, your job is not easy either. You have a lot to do at home and Bob can't be there to help because he has to earn a living. And you kids sound like you would like some things to be different too. It must be hard for you, Tommy, to be catching so much flack these days. I think this also makes it hard for you to have fun at home too, Sissy."

She looked at each person briefly and was sure to make eye contact. "There seems to be a lot going on. What I would like to do is talk with you together and then see the parents for a while and then maybe you kids alone, to hear your sides of the story. I think we are going to need to understand a lot of things to see why this is happening. I can hear, Tommy, that it is hard for you to be living in this family right now and that it is hard for your parents to have you. Also, as you have gotten older, it may be that you have thought you should be treated a little differently by your folks. What I would like everyone to do is to think about how each of you, if you could, would change the other family members so that you would be happier in the family. I will want everyone to tell me that and I want you all to listen to what the others have to say.

Ms. Fargo began the process she had outlined, trying to

make sure everyone was heard. As the therapy continued she saw all the family members alone and then together as a unit. She would speak with them and ask them how things could be different and what they could do to help bring about changes. Slowly, with her help, family members began to communicate more clearly with one another and to see how the behavior of each family member influenced the other family members. Sometimes they were not at all aware that changes in one person meant changes in the whole family. They explored how difficult it was to change one's image in an ongoing group; the family seemed to have settled into a rut of treating each other in a prescribed way. Tommy especially felt this; no matter what he did, he was always treated the same.

The discussions with Ms. Fargo focused attention on the feelings of being "trapped" in a web of unchanging relationships. It was boring and frustrating. However, the Davises found that they all shared these feelings. Over a series of sessions they discussed how they could change their present situation. They experimented with new behaviors and slowly they began enjoying being together as a family.

## SOCIAL DYNAMICS OF FAMILY THERAPY

Family therapy can represent an interesting case of group therapy. Certainly, it is a type of group therapy; there may be anywhere from two to ten clients, though in most cases we are dealing with a group of four or five. However, in the group therapy discussed in Chapter 3, we were dealing with a group of strangers. Further, those individuals would be unlikely to see one another after the therapy session. Hence, such issues as deindividuation and conformity based on fear of being rejected by the group were important.

In family therapy, we are dealing with a group of individuals who are well acquainted with one another. They see one another after every session and they will continue to interact long after they terminate therapy. Thus, we are unlikely to be concerned with deindividuation or the *stranger passant* phenomenon. While the therapy situation may be somewhat strange to the family members, they have few uncertainties about how to act in the group (the family) and they have little fear of being rejected by the group. Thus, the pressures for conformity will be different than in the group of strangers.

While some of the dynamics present in group therapy may not be as readily evident in family therapy, there are many similarities between the two.Contagion can occur in both. Each member of the Davis family entered therapy with a desire to express anger over past events. However, they all continued to repress this anger until Mr. Davis expressed his dissatisfaction with his son Tommy. Then the other members also began voicing their own anger. Modeling behavior is also likely to occur in family therapy. In the present example, it is interesting to note that each member of the Davis family imitated Ms. Fargo to some degree. Mr. Davis adopted Ms. Fargo's "listening mannerisms"; he leaned forward in his chair and nodded his head slowly when some other member of the family spoke. Mrs. Davis attempted to respond to her family by saying how their actions made her feel rather than telling them how they should behave. She noticed and admired this behavior in Ms. Fargo. Sissy, who had previously been very quick to criticize and slow to praise, began to respond in a more supportive manner. She had been very impressed by the way Ms. Fargo responded to the family in a positive rather than negative, critical manner. The Davis family also made some "risky" decisions as a group. For example, they encouraged Mr. Davis to spend some of the family savings on the motorcycle he had always wanted rather than take the more conservative course of action and save all the money for Tom's college education. Thus, some of the phenomena that occur in group therapy are likely to occur in family therapy while others are not.

Looking at the example we can also see that there are events that may be found in family therapy that are not so apparent in a therapy group made up of strangers. It is to some of these that we now turn our attention.

*Norms and roles.* Looking at the opening example, we can see a certain pattern in the way the Davis family discussed topics. In almost every case, Mr. Davis spoke first. He was usually the one responsible for bringing up new issues. He brought up the family problems with Tom. He raised the issue of the family finances; he began the discussion on the lack of closeness within the family. After Mr. Davis defined the issue and took a stand, Mrs. Davis often spoke next. Her response was generally to echo and support the position of her husband. Tommy or Sissy spoke next. Rarely would they directly contradict their father even when pressed by Ms. Fargo. In the one case when Tom strongly disagreed with his father, he was quickly rebuked by both his father and mother. Ms. Fargo pointed out this pattern to the Davises. She asked Mrs. Davis if she generally found herself in such close agreement with her husband. After some thought, Mrs. Davis stated, "I generally try to agree with Bob. I think it is a wife's duty to support her husband. What kind of image would it project if I took different positions from Bob?"

This statement reflected the norms and role expectations that characterized the Davis family. Whenever individuals form groups, they develop rules that govern specific behaviors. These rules or **norms** "specify *what* must, or must not, be done when" (Steiner, 1972, p. 171). These rules apply to everyone in the group and are generally unwritten. Their purpose is to help the group function more smoothly. For example, a norm in many groups traveling by ship is that women and children will enter life rafts first if the ship encounters difficulty. If this rule is followed, the abandoning of ship will occur with more order than if everyone rushed to be first into the life raft. Further, this norm is unwritten but anyone violating it will be severely rebuked.

Looking at the Davis family, we can see that one norm was that Mr. Davis should be allowed to talk first and the other members of the family should support him. This norm was unwritten but it did apply to all members of the family. If anyone violated this norm, they were scolded. In the example, the norm had both positive and negative effects. On the positive side, the norm gave order to the Davis' conversations. It ensured that they would not be constantly faced by the problems of everyone talking at once, nor would they face the turmoil of open and heated arguments between family members. On the negative side, the norm inhibited open expression of feeling and spontaneity. It proved to be one of the reasons for a lack of real cohesiveness within the family and much of the therapy was devoted to changing the norm to allow for more open communication among the family members.

The concept of **role** is closely related to norms. A role defines the obligations and expectations of an individual in a certain position (Goffman, 1961). In essence, a role is a set of norms that applies to a person in a particular position. For example, Mr. Davis occupied the position of father in the family. He felt that the norms governing that role required him to be the leader, to supply the family with food, clothing, and shelter, to define what was "right and wrong" for the family, and to be the individual who ultimately made the decisions for the family. Mrs. Davis had a clear view of the norms governing her role as wife. The overriding norm was that she was supposed to support her husband as this was a "wife's duty."

Individuals often occupy many roles at any time. Oftentimes the requirements of these multiple roles may be at odds and create **role conflict** for the individual. This clearly was the case for Mrs. Davis, who reported feeling "torn between her children and her husband." Actually she felt torn between the view of her role of wife and mother. As a wife she felt it her duty to support her husband; as a mother she felt she should nurture and support her children. Hence, she was in terrible conflict when her children held different positions on issues than her husband.

As the therapy sessions progressed, Ms. Fargo was able to obtain a better understanding of the Davis family and the problems that faced them by discovering the norms and role expectations that existed within the family. She saw how the role conflicts created problems for Mrs. Davis and how some of the family norms created a communication barrier between the family members. During the therapy sessions she pointed out to the Davises that norms are developed by the group and they can be changed by the group. She tried to show them that norms should aid the group functions rather than hinder it. During the therapy sessions she had the Davises experiment with different norms to see which were most helpful to the family.

*Aggression.* Throughout the sessions, there were periodic bursts of anger and aggression. In the first session, Tommy grew angry when he heard his father discussing his disobedience and moodiness. Tom sat and listened for a period of time and then tried to give his side of the story. Each time he began to talk his father would break in. Finally, Tom could take no more and he exploded, "Will you be quiet and let me talk! You never let me talk."

Social psychologists have conducted numerous studies on aggression over the last half century. Out of the hundreds of experiments two major theories have emerged to explain the causes of human aggression. The frustration-aggression theory was developed by a group of Yale psychologists (Dollard, Doob, Miller, Mowrer, and Sears, 1939). The theory states that "aggression is always the consequence of frustration" and "frustration always leads to some form of aggression" (p. 1). Dollard et al. defined frustration as an interference with a behavior sequence and aggression as a behavior whose goal is the injury of the target. Essentially the theory stated that people aggress when they are blocked from doing something that they either want to do or are in the process of doing.

This description fits the situation that led to Tom's anger. Tom wanted to talk and, in fact, made several attempts to do so. However, each time he was thwarted by his father's interruption. In this situation, he aggressed directly against his father. However, at other times Tom aimed his aggression at his sister. Tom's mother complained that he often seemed to try and hurt Sissy just "out of meanness." Mrs. Davis pointed out that Sissy did nothing to instigate his behavior.

According to frustration-aggression theory, this situation would constitute a case of displaced aggression. Dollard et al. hypothesized that the most preferred target of aggression would be the thwarter. However, there are times when the thwarter may not be available to serve as a target or the angered individual inhibits aggressing against the thwarter. In the case of Tom, when he was at home he dared not aggress directly against his father for fear of quick and severe punishment. When this happens, frustration-aggression is redirected onto some other available and safer target. In the case of Tom, this other target was Sissy. Hence, Ms. Fargo attempted to point out that Tom's behavior toward Sissy may not have been due to "just plain meanness." He may have been displacing his aggression from his father to his sister.

One other concept from the frustration-aggression theory is important for our present discussion. After Tom's outburst in therapy, Ms. Fargo asked him how he felt. You may have been surprised by his answer as he stated, "I'm a little shaken because I can't ever remember attacking my father like that. However, I've got to admit that I actually feel pretty good—like I just got a tremendous load off my shoulders." According to frustration-aggression theorists, Tom was experiencing catharsis. Dollard et al. stated that any act of aggression should reduce the aggressor's arousal and reduce his instigation to further aggression. In addition, Bramel, Taub, and Blum (1968) found that subjects reported "feeling good" after aggressing. As we pointed out in Chapter 3, there is still some disagreement as to whether or not aggression actually results in catharsis or increases the likelihood of future aggression. There does seem to be some agreement, however, that the act of aggression may reduce an individual's arousal and lead to "good feelings." Of course, this could only result when aggression is not followed by anxiety or guilt.

A second theory of aggression states that aggression is a learned behavior. (See Chapter 2.) This social learning approach (Bandura and Walters, 1963) suggests that there are two processes by which the individual learns to be aggressive. The first is positive reinforcement. Individuals are often rewarded for acting aggressively. A child may beat up another to obtain a desired object; a young football player may receive praise from his coach for making a particularly vicious tackle; a neglected family member may receive attention when he or she aggresses against a brother or sister. Thus, the individual learns that "aggression pays" and this behavior will be used as long as reinforcement is forthcoming.

Modeling is a second mechanism through which aggression is learned. As we discussed in Chapter 2, individuals imitate those people whom they admire and/or see as successful. An aggressive model which demonstrates that aggression is a useful behavior also teaches exactly how one can aggress. Wolfgang (1966) pointed out that we are surrounded by examples that violence is "good." Our national security is based on our ability to aggress and violence permeates our advertising and television programming; there is one act of violence on television every sixteen minutes and by the age of sixteen, the average adolescent has witnessed 13,000 murders on television (Walters and Malamud, 1975).

Modeling is an important concept when trying to understand the behavior of family members. Mr. and Mrs. Davis were very concerned with Tom's aggressive behavior. Mr. Davis complained, "Spanking does no good. I spank him frequently and sometimes I whip him so hard he can't sit down. Then the next thing I know he's back hitting his sister or picking on one of the neighbor's children. I just can't understand him—he doesn't seem to learn." This latter statement may be very inaccurate; Tommy may be learning very well. In Tom's eyes, Mr. Davis is a strong and successful person. He often is able to get family members to act the way he wants by yelling at them or spanking them. Thus, if aggression is such a successful behavior for Mr. Davis, why shouldn't it be as successful for Tom? Mr. Davis serves as a model for his son and much of Tom's aggressive behavior may be the result of trying to imitate his father.

*Group decision making.*   During the fourth session, Mr. Davis suggested that they have two sessions a week rather than the current one a week. When he asked Ms. Fargo if that would be possible, she said it would be but suggested that the whole family should be involved in the decision since they would all be affected by it. Mr. Davis then turned to the other family members and told them all the reasons he felt a second session would be beneficial for the group. After finishing, he stated, "Can you all see why the extra session would be good at this point? Are there any strong objections?" No one responded and Mr. Davis took this silence to mean that they all agreed. Two weekly sessions were planned. However, the sessions that followed this decision did not go smoothly. Tom and Sissy participated little in the discussions and Mrs. Davis missed two sessions because "she was not feeling well." Mr. Davis was per- plexed. He had suggested the extra sessions because he felt that they had been making a great deal of progress. "What's going on?" he asked at one of the later sessions. At this point, Ms. Fargo suggested that they discuss their feelings about the extra session. Mrs. Davis hesitantly responded. "I felt the extra session would be a good idea. We were progressing well up to that point and we were working together. I guess I was a little upset at the way the decision to have the extra sessions was made. I just didn't feel that I really had any input into it. I had some concerns about giving the extra time and money and I never really got a chance to talk about them." Sissy and Tom reported similar feelings. Mr. Davis responded that he was just trying to do the thing that was best for everyone and that the other family members seemed to agree with his reasons for wanting the extra sessions. The remainder of this session was devoted to discussing the importance of involving all the group members when making a group decision.

In Chapter 1 we saw how during World War II Kurt Lewin was concerned with issues of group decision making. The American housewife did not use the abundant supply of beef entrails and the government embarked on an extensive media campaign to convince the housewife to use these meats in lieu of the scarce more popular cuts. Lewin felt that this media method would not be successful because it was aimed at the individual housewife rather than at the group to which she belonged and the media campaign did not allow the housewife to discuss or participate in the decision to change her behavior.

In order to demonstrate the importance of these variables, Lewin formed groups of thirteen to seventeen housewives. Half the groups heard a lecture on the advantages of using beef entrails. The other half were given the opportunity to discuss their feelings about using the entrails and to vote on a proposal to serve at least one meal of entrails a week to their families. One week later all the women were interviewed. Only 10 percent of the women in the lecture groups had actually served entrails while 52 percent of the women in the group discussion condition served the entrails. Additional research (Pennington, Harary, and Bass, 1958) demonstrated that group discussion is important if one wishes group members to commit themselves to a group decision

During the discussion of decision making, Mr. Davis raised the issue of whether or not it was always better to have the group involved in the decision-making process. He recalled several times when the family had made "bad" decisions as a group. He stated that in many of those cases, one person could probably have made a better decision than the family did. Ms. Fargo acknowledged that this may happen but suggested that the way in which the group decision is made may be as important as having everyone involved in the decision.

This point is clearly made by Irving Janis' (1971) discussion of the dynamics involved in the decision by the Kennedy administration to conduct the Bay of Pigs invasion. On April 17, 1966, a group of 1,400 Cuban exiles landed at the Bay of Pigs, Cuba. Their mission was to establish a beachhead at the Bay and then lead a rebellion to over-throw Premier Fidel Castro. This mission had been carefully planned by the Central Intelligence Agency and approved by President John Kennedy. Despite being heavily armed and having received a great deal of intelligence information on the Cuban army, the invasion collapsed almost as soon as it began. The Cuban army was well prepared for the invasion and the Cuban people were not willing to join a rebellion. The entire force was surrounded by the Cuban army which killed or captured every one of the invaders.

Many people raised the question of how the Kennedy administration could have approved such a faulty and ill-conceived plan. Janis (1971; 1972) suggested that a condition called **groupthink** may have characterized the Kennedy decision makers. According to Janis, groupthink results when group members become so concerned with maintaining a high degree of group consensus and cohesiveness that they fail to critically evaluate ideas. Groupthink is most likely to result in groups where there is a strong and respected leader and where there are strong pressures toward conformity. Groupthink often leads the group to quickly adopt the position of the leader without serious question or evaluation. This may result in the group making an inferior decision.

In order to avoid groupthink, Janis suggests that the leader should avoid stating a preference. Instead he should encourage group members to consider all alternatives and even to play the role of "devil's advocate." There should also be a continual reassessment of new information.

Ms. Fargo pointed out to Mr. Davis how groupthink may occur in a family. The family is often a cohesive group with a strong leader. Family members are concerned about keeping a degree of unanimity and, hence, there are pressures to conform. Thus, these concerns and pressures may result in family members failing to critically evaluate suggestions and agreeing simply to preserve consensus.

## APPLICATIONS IN CLINICAL PRACTICE

In the past ten years, there has been a great increase in the popularity of family therapy. Family theorists have generated a group of theories which conceive of families not just as groups affected by the pathology of an individual (a position originally held by some psychodynamics theorists) but as functioning "systems" each of which has its own norms (often called family rules), roles, and patterns of behavior. The basic characteristic of a system or a set of interlocking roles (roles which cannot exist without the presence of other roles) is that change in any individual will change the entire system in some way. Intervention, therefore, has to be at the system level or changes will snowball through the family unit creating more stress and confusion. In other words, the modification of one family member's behavior will make it difficult for all to function in the ways they have in the past. In the case of the Davises, as Tommy grew into adolescence and desired to have more independence in his family, his role began to change. He did not want to be treated as "Mommy's little boy." He began to fight frequently at school so that she would have to see his role differently. Mrs. Davis, however, still saw Tommy as her little boy who was now acting like a "bad" boy instead of the model child she expected him to be. Since what she expected from Tommy and what she observed in him were not the same behaviors, she had to change her behavior to treat him differently in an attempt to change his behavior. This also produced a change in Mr. Davis' behavior. Everyone in the system was affected by the change that began with Tommy's desire for independence.

The systems dynamics which were responsible for the Davis' family problems, were also present in the intervention made by Ms. Fargo. If she were to attempt to change Tommy into a good boy, this might jeopardize Sissy's role as the "good little girl." Sissy might then change her behavior, which would in turn have complications for her parents. It is essential in working with the family system that the therapist be aware of the force of the roles already existing in the family and the patterns of communication between members.

This last point about patterns of communication is quite important. It is not uncommon for family members to communicate to one another in a way that cannot easily be understood by others. Different family members see the world in different ways as a function of their roles in the family and also because each person's personality is unique. As a result, family members frequently misunderstand the intent of the statements or behaviors of other family members. Often, it is mistakenly assumed that because of their intimate relationship, family members naturally understand one another. This is, however, often far from true. In the Davis' case, Mrs. Davis did not understand that Tom's behavior was intended to force her to see him more as an adult. She probably thought that he was fighting at school to make her angry or for some other reason. It seems clear from the session in the example that neither of them had a clear understanding of what the other intended.

There are two major theories of the family; both are clearly social psychological in nature. The first theory views families in terms of the role relationships of family members. Ackerman (1958) believes that the "social role" a person has in the family is a result of the interaction of the forces in the family and the individual's own personality. Systems theory, the second major family theory, conceives of the entire family as a system with members playing roles which are functions of the forces of the system. In the first instance an understanding of the individual's personality is necessary to aid in the treatment of the family. In systems theory, however, it is believed that certain forces exist in the family structure which mold the responses of the individuals involved. Within systems theory, different theorists view these forces as being manifest in a number of different ways, most notably through the process of communication between family members.

Some theorists believe that certain types of communications convey more than one meaning simultaneously. An example of this is the phenomenon of the "double bind" (Bateson, Jackson, Haley, and Weakland, 1968). In a double bind, a message is given to do two contradictory things at the same time, creating confusion in the person who receives the communication. In the case of the Davises, Mr. Davis may expect Tommy to behave, yet he condones fighting as being "manly." So at the same time, he may be telling Tommy to fight and to behave; Tommy, then, cannot succeed in his father's eyes no matter what he does. These double messages are often conveyed by incongruent verbal and nonverbal communications. (Mr. Davis may say not to fight, but he has a smile on his face communicating that it is OK to fight. This confusion in communication produces poorly functioning families with rigid rule systems. The major goal of the therapist would then be to clarify the communications between family members. The incongruity of a mixed message precipitates stress felt by family members and encourages the system to break down or rigidly enforce its rules at the expense of some of its members. In the case of the Davises, Tommy wanted his behavior at school to communicate that he is a man and not a little boy. Mr. Davis saw this behavior as disobedience, and he took repressive measures to keep the family in order ("don't get in trouble at school, or don't disappoint your mother!"). These rigid measures create stress for Tommy who must, then, stop, or if the pressure is too great, find a way to leave the family, perhaps by escalating his communication by increasing his acting out behavior.

In addition to clarifying communications, the therapist may make the family rules explicit so that everyone knows what they are and why they exist. Many times the family norms are observed both by children and adults even though they do not know how they were established or why. Frequently, the rules are unspoken and unclear until one has been broken.

Part of the reason that clear communication may be

important in the family system is that it will allow family members to express to one another what they think and feel. For them it initiates responses from others in the family. These responses, if positive, validate their existence in the family. This validation, according to Satir (1972), is necessary if the family is to be healthy. A function of the therapist is to ensure that family members are validated and acknowledged by other family members, and by the therapist. In the case example, Ms. Fargo was careful to ask everyone for his or her opinion and respected what she heard from them. She did not discount anyone or cut anyone off.

The therapist can model for the family in the sessions how to face the hostility which might exist between parents or between parents and children. Showing them how to be angry and be heard without hurting each other facilitates further communication and validation. The therapist can also model how to make decisions in such a way that everyone in the family feels they have some presence and power. In other words, this allows them to feel good about themselves in the family, even if they do not always get their own way.

The strategies for therapy mentioned above are some of many that are implied by theories of family dynamics. Many, however, can also be understood in terms of how they affect the social psychological process of the family and of the relationship between the family and the therapist.

When the family therapist helps the members of a family to explicate the family rules, he or she is getting them in touch with the stress which occurs when the family norms are violated. When the family members can see this stress and share their experience of it, they may begin to see that they can change the roles they play. Also, the unwritten rules of the family are brought to light and the reason for their existence can be evaluated. Many of the norms may have outlived their usefulness but, because of force of habit, family members still abide by them. When this is explicit, the rules can be changed to meet everyone's needs more fully. An example of this sort of situation relates to family myths. Family myths are unwritten, covert expectations that were created long ago in the family. Often, no one knows when they started or why. For the Davises there was a family myth that "men lead the family, so men speak first." They may not know why that is so in their family or when they started to believe it, but everyone believes the myth and follows the rule.

In addition to revealing the family rules and norms, the therapist can help family members validate one another. Validation is the expression of feelings about other family members. It is the acknowledgment of their existence, letting them know their impact on others in the family. In social psychological terms, this validation through expression of feelings allows family members to express their good feelings about others, and also vent frustrations they may feel. The reduction of the level of frustration experienced by family members may lead to the reduction of the overall level of aggression expressed. In addition, as was the case in the treatment of couples, a good therapist will model for the family how to constructively express their aggressive feelings and how to argue in a constructive fashion. The process begins when the therapist listens carefully to all members of the family in the first session. Ms. Fargo was very careful to make sure that she had at least asked everyone in the family to speak in the first session, to talk about what was on their minds. Once the tone was set, validation for people's feelings could continue throughout the sessions with family members validating each other.

Another major function of the therapist is to clarify the communciations between family members. This is frequently the most difficult task for the therapist. The first step of the process is for a therapist to ensure that he or she understands what each family member is trying to communicate. Some family members may be more verbal than others, more intelligent than others, more emotional or sensitive than others. The therapist must listen and attempt to understand. The second step is to translate the communication to other family members in a way that they can understand. In this way the communication can be clarified. Then the therapist must begin the process of teaching the family members how to understand one another. An effective therapist according to Bandler, Grinder, and Satir (1976) must first serve to connect family members, then translate for them, and finally show them how to communicate directly with one another. For instance, Ms. Fargo listened closely to everyone in an effort to identify that Tommy was trying to communicate to the family that he was grown up. She then translated this message so that the other family members would understand. ("Perhaps when Tom is fighting in school he is trying to tell you that he can stand on his own two feet and take care of himself, that he is not just Mamma's little boy any more.") Ms. Fargo tried to get each family member to understand what others were trying to say by asking them to be direct and by repeating what they heard others say. In this way family members could hear whether they had communicated clearly to one another.

When communications are more direct and explicit, decisions are much easier to make and family members feel more a part of the process. As shown in Lewin's experiment, when discussion and participation occur, the decisions tend to be followed up more by appropriate behaviors. If the Davises could all participate in the decision of what might be done, the family members would be more likely to go along with it, including Tommy who would feel validated by his own participation.

Finally, the effect of clear communications is also to break up the process of groupthink. If each member of the family feels he or she can express how he or she feels to the others and work out any differences that they may have, the effects of groupthink will be minimized and the family will be aware of the decisions they make and feel as though they are supported by the other family members. The therapist must be sure that the family members are not only clear about what they are trying to communicate to the others, but that they clearly understand what the others are trying to communicate to them.

## CONCLUSION

In many ways, the family therapist serves as a consultant to the family, almost as a psychologist may serve as consultant to a large organization. The consultant makes explicit to the members just how the organization works and tries to promote an atmosphere of free and clear communication which gives every member a feeling of belonging, but also a feeling of freedom and autonomy. It is also crucial, however, for therapists to realize that when intervening in any system, family or group, they become a part of the system, subject to many of the same forces which are exerted upon family and group members. A good therapist must use his or her own sensitivity to be sure not to get swallowed up by the process that is to be understood and revealed. It is often easier for a consultant to see this than a clinician, who may feel obligated to "help" the family, even at his or her own personal expense. This desire to help may interfere with the ability to serve as a connector, translator and consultant.

It seems obvious from this chapter that social psychological forces play a large part in the functioning of family systems and in the performance of effective family intervention. Understanding these forces allows the therapist to have one more sensitive instrument to use in the examination and treatment of families.

## SELECTED READINGS

Bandler, Richard; Grinder, John; and Satir, Virginia. *Changing With Families.* Palo Alto: Science and Behavior Books, 1976.

Erickson, Gerald, and Hogan, Terrence (eds.). *Family*

*Therapy: An Introduction to Therapy and Technique.* Monterey, Calif.: Brooks/Cole Publishing Co., 1975.

Foley, Vincent. *An Introduction to Family Therapy.* New York: Grune & Stratton, 1974.

Guerin, Philip (ed.). *Family Therapy: Theory and Practice.* New York: Gardner Press, 1976.

# Chapter 6

# Epilogue

This book has been about the relationship between clinical psychology and social psychology; about opening up a new level of discourse and understanding between two previously exclusive disciplines in psychology. It is, at best, just a beginning of what we hope will be a new spirit of sharing and cooperation between two fields that study human behavior. This volume represents the collaboration of a clinically-oriented social psychologist and a socially-oriented clinical psychologist. Our ability to share with each other to produce this volume demonstrated to us just how well the two fields fit together.

While writing this book, neither of us has ever been at a loss to comment upon what the other has said or written. The process for us has been one of continual insight and revelation as we have shared our views on the nature of the universe from our own disciplines. Our excitement has grown as the writing continued. Each of us has found that there already exists theory and even some research in areas we thought to be virgin territory in our various fields. We have emerged with a greater respect for the other's field, and a greater insight into the process of our own.

In the development of any new interdisciplinary field, there is a certain openmindedness which is required. This seems especially necessary between two fields related so centrally to human behavior and interaction. In the case of clinical psychology, there have traditionally existed not only conceptual differences among members of the discipline, but political separation on the basis of these differences (e.g., behaviorists versus psychoanalysts). The application of social psychological theory to this field may be difficult, unless these differences can be put aside. It is important, now, however, to do so, as the mutual contribution born out of the cooperation is too significant to ignore. We hope that others will follow us and expand the research base to add additional significance to the endeavor. You, the reader, can learn from this work, not just the fruits of our cooperation, but a perspective of broadmindedness which is essential to the progress of psychology in the era of specialization and territoriality. The combination of disciplines we examine here is probably but one of many that can be and should be explored by this generation of psychologists. Now that disciplines have attained their identities it is important that they use them in cooperation with others to obtain the broadest understanding of human behavior.

# References

Ackerman, N. *The Psychodynamics of Family Life.* New York: Basic Books, 1958.

Allen, V. L. "Situational factors in conformity." In L. Berkowitz (ed.). *Advances in Experimental Social Psychology,* Vol. 2. New York: Academic Press, 1965, pp. 133–170.

Argyle, M. "Social pressures in public and private situations." *Journal of Abnormal and Social Psychology,* 1957, *54,* 172–175.

Aronson, E., and Mills, J. "The effect of severity of initiation on liking for a group." *Journal of Abnormal and Social Psychology,* 1959, *59,* 177–181.

Asch, S. "Effects of group pressure upon the modification and distortion of judgment." In H. Guetzkow (ed.). *Groups, Leadership, and Men.* Pittsburgh: Carnegie Press, 1951.

Bach, G., and Deutsch, R. M. *Pairing.* New York: Avon Books, 1970.

Bach, G., and Goldberg, H. *Creative Aggression.* New York: Avon Books, 1974.

Bach, G., and Wyden, P. *The Intimate Enemy.* New York: Avon Books, 1968.

Bandler, R., and Grinder, J. *The Structure of Magic.* Palo Alto: Science and Behavior Books, 1975.

Bandler, R.; Grinder, J.; and Satir, V. *Changing with Families.* Palo Alto: Science and Behavior Books, 1976.

Bandura, A. *Principles of Behavior Modification.* New York: Holt, Rinehart & Winston, 1969.

Bandura, A.; Ross, D.; and Ross, S. "Transmission of aggression through imitation of aggressive models." *Journal of Abnormal and Social Psychology,* 1961, *63,* 575–582.

_____. "Imitation of film-mediated aggressive models." *Journal of Abnormal and Social Psychology*, 1963, 66, 3–11 (a).

_____. "Vicarious reinforcement and imitative learning." *Journal of Abnormal and Social Psychology*, 1963, 67, 601–607 (b).

Bandura, A., and Walters, R. *Social Learning and Personality Development.* New York: Holt, Rinehart & Winston, 1963.

Bateson, G; Jackson, P. M.; Halez, J.; and Weddand, B. "Toward a theory of Schizophrenia." In D, Jackson (ed.). *Communication, Family and Marriage.* Palo Alto: Science and Behavior Books, 1968.

Benne, K. D.; Bradford, L. P.; Gibb, J. R.; and Lippitt, R. O. (eds.). *The Laboratory Method of Changing and Learning.* Palo Alto: Science and Behavior Books, 1975.

Birdwhistell, R. L. *Introduction of Kinestics.* Louisville, Ky.: University of Louisville Press, Foreign Services Institute, 1952.

Blascovich, J; Ginsburg, G.; and Howe, R. "Blackjack and the risky shift: II Monetary Stakes" *Journal of Experimental Social Psychology*, 1975, 11, 224–232.

Bossard, J., "Residential propinquity as a factor in marriage selection." *American Journal of Sociology*, 1932, 38, 219–224.

Bramel, D.; Taub, B.; and Blum, B. "An observer's reaction to the suffering of his enemy." *Journal of Personality and Social Psychology*, 1968, 8, 384–392.

Brehm, J. W. *A Theory of Psychological Reactance.* New York: Academic Press, 1966.

Brown, B. "The effects of need to maintain face on interpersonal bargaining." *Journal of Experimental Social Psychology*, 1968, 4, 107–122.

Burnstein, E., and Vinokur, A. "Testing two classes of theories about group induced shifts in individual choice." *Journal of Experimental Social Psychology,* 1973, *9,* 123–137.

Byrne, D. "Interpersonal attraction and attitude similarity." *Journal of Abnormal and Social Psychology* 1961 *62,* 713–715.

_____.*The Attraction Paradigm.* New York: Academic Press, 1971.

Byrne, D.; Glore, G.; and Worchel, P. "The effect of economic similarity-dissimilarity on interpersonal attraction. "*Journal of Personality and Social Psychology,* 1966, *4,* 220–224.

Byrne, D., Griffitt, W.; and Stefaniak, D. "Attraction and similarity of personality characteristics." *Journal of Personality and Social Psychology,* 1967, *5,* 82–90.

Caplow, T. "A theory of coalitions in the triad." *American Sociological Review,* 1956, *21,* 489–493.

Chen, S. "Social modification of the activity of ants in nestbuilding." *Physiological Zoology,* 1937, *10,* 420–436.

Cooper, J. Unpublished Manuscript, Princeton University. Princeton, N. J., 1979.

Corsini, R. (ed.). *Current Psychotherapies.* Itasca, Ill.: F. E. Peacock Publishers, 1973.

Deutsch, M. *The Resolution of Conflict.* New Haven: Yale University Press, 1973.

Deutsch, M., and Gerard, H. "A study of normative and informational influence upon individual judgment." *Journal of Abnormal and Social Psychology,* 1955, *51,* 629–636.

Deutsch, M., and Krauss, R. M. "The effect of threat upon interpersonal bargaining." *Journal of Abnormal and Social Psychology,* 1960, *61,* 181–189.

Dittes, J., and Kelley, H. H. "Effects of different conditions of acceptance upon conformity to group norms." *Journal of Abnormal and Social Psychology,* 1956, *53,* 100–107.

Dollard, J.; Dobb, L.; Miller, N; Mowrer, O.; and Sears. R. *Frustration and Aggression.* New Haven: Yale University Press, 1939.

Ekman, P. "Differential communication of affect by head and body cues." *Journal of Personality and Social Psychology,* 1965, 2, 726–735.

Ekman, P., and Friesen, W. "Nonverbal leakage and clues to deception." *Psychiatry,* 1969, 32, 88–106.

Ellis, A. "Rational psychotherapy." *Journal of General Psychology,* 1958, 59, 35–43.

Erickson, G., and Hagan, T. (eds.). *Family Therapy: An Introduction to Theory and Technique.* Monterey, Calif.: Brooks/Cole Publishing Co., 1975.

Exline, R., and Winters, L. "Affective relations and mutual glances." In S. S. Tompkins and C. E. Izard (eds.). *Affect Cognition and Personality.* New York: Springer, 1965.

Feshbach, S. "The stimulating versus cathartic effects of a vicarious aggressive activity." *Journal of Abnormal and Social Psychology,* 1961, 63, 381–385.

Festinger, L. *A Theory of Cognitive Dissonance.* Stanford, Calif.: Stanford University Press, 1957.

Festinger, L.; Schachter, S.; and Back, K. *Social Pressures in Informal Groups: A Study of a Housing Community.* New York: Harper, 1950.

Foleg, V. *An Introduction to Family Therapy.* New York: Grune & Stratton, 1975.

Freedman, J. L., and Dobb, A. N. *Deviancy: The Psychology of Being Different.* New York: Academic Press, 1968.

Garfield, S. *Clinical Psychology: The Study of Personality and Behavior.* Chicago: Aldine, 1974.

Gerard, H. B., and Mathewson, G. "The effects of severity of initiation on liking for a group: A replication." *Journal of Experimental Social Psychology,* 1966, 2, 278–287.

Gibb, J. R. "The Tra...ing Group." In Benne, Bradford, Gibb, and Lippitt (eds.). *The Laboratory Method of Changing & Learning.* Palo Alto: Science and Behavior Books, 1975.

Goffman, E. *The Presentation of Self in Everyday Life.* Garden City, N.Y.: Doubleday, 1959.

_____. *Asylums.* Garden City, N.Y.: Doubleday, 1961.

Goldfried, M., and Davison, G. *Clinical Behavior Therapy.* New York: Holt, Rinehart and Winston, 1976.

Golembiewski, R. T., and Blumberg, A. (eds.). *Sensitivity Training and the Laboratory Approach.* Itasca, Ill.: F. E. Peacock Publishers, 1970.

Guerin, P. (ed.). *Family Therapy: Theory and Practice:* New York: Gardner Press, 1976.

Hall, E. T. *The Hidden Dimension.* Garden City, N.Y.: Doubleday, 1966.

Hammock, T., and Brehm, J. W. "The attractiveness of choice alternatives when freedom to choose is eliminated by a social agent." *Journal of Personality,* 1966, *34,* 546–554.

Hess, E. "The pupil responds to changes in attitude as well as illumination." *Scientific American,* 1965, *212,* 46–54.

Janis, I. "Groupthink." *Psychology Today,* 1971, *5,* 43–46.

_____. *Victims of Groupthink: A Psychological Study of Foreign Policy Decisions and Fiascoes.* Boston: Houghton Mifflin, 1972.

Jones, E. E., and Nisbett, R. E. *The Actor and the Observer: Divergent Perceptions of the Causes of Behavior.* Morristown, N.J.: General Learning Press, 1971.

Koch-Sheras, P. R. *"Dealing with Past Hurts,"* Paper presented at American Psychological Association Convention, Toronto, Canada, 1978.

Lavey, L. "Factors affecting cooperation in the Prisoner's Dilemma." *Behavioral Science,* 1965, *10,* 26–38.

Lett, E.; Clark, W.; and Altman, I. *A Propositional Inventory of Research on Interpersonal Distance.* Bethesda, Md.: Naval Medical Research Institute, 1969.

Lewin, K. *A Dynamic Theory of Personality.* New York: McGraw-Hill, 1935.

_____. *Field Theory in Social Science.* New York: Harper, 1951.

_____. "Forces behind food habits and methods of change." *Bulletin of the National Research Council,* 1943, *108,* 35–65.

Lieberman, M. A.; Yalom, I. D.; and Miles, M. B. *Encounter Groups: First Facts.* New York: Basic Books, 1973.

Lott, A. J., and Lott, B. E. "A learning theory approach to interpersonal attitudes." In A. G. Greenwald, T. C. Brock, and T. McOstrom (eds.). *Psychological Foundations of Attitudes.* New York: Academic Press, 1968.

Luce, R. D., and Raiffa, H. *Games and Decisions.* New York: Wiley, 1957.

McArthur, L. "The how and what of why! Some determinants and consequences of casual attribution." *Journal of Personality and Social Psychology,* 1972, 22, 171–193.

Mehrabian, A. *Nonverbal Communication.* Chicago: Aldine, 1972.

Meichenbaum, D. *Cognitive-Behavior Modification.* New York: Plenum Press, 1977.

Mikulas, W. *Behavior Modification: An Overview.* New York: Harper & Row, Publishers, 1972.

Morse, S., and Watson, R., Jr. *Psychotherapies.* New York: Holt, Rinehart & Winston, 1977.

Perls, F. S. *Gestalt Therapy Verbatim.* Lafayette, Calif.: Real People Press, 1969.

Pruitt, D. "Definition of the Situation as a determinant of international action." In H. Kelman (Ed.). *International Behavior.* New York: Holt, Rinehart & Winston, 1965.

Raven, B. H. "Social influence on opinions and the communication of related content." *Journal of Abnormal and Social Psychology,* 1959, 58, 119–128.

Rogers, C. *Client-Centered Therapy.* Boston: Houghton Mifflin, 1965.

Rosenthal, R., and Jacobson, L. *Pygmalion in the Classroom: Teacher Expectation and Pupils' Intellectual*

*Development.* New York: Holt, Rinehart & Winston, 1968.

Sager, C. J. *Marriage Controls and Couple Therapy.* New York: Brunner/Mazel, 1976.

Sager, C. J., and Kaplan, H. S. (eds.). *Progress in Group and Family Therapy.* New York: Brunner/Mazel, 1972.

Satir, V. *People Makery.* Palo Alto: Science and Behavior Books, 1972.

Schachter, S. "Deviation, rejection and communication." *Journal of Abnormal and Social Psychology,* 1951, *46,* 190–207.

Schachter, S., and Singer, J. "Cognitive, social and physiological determinants of emotional state." *Psychological Review,* 1962, *69,* 379–399.

Schlenker, B.; Helm, B.; and Tedeschi, J. "The effects of personality and situational variables on behavioral trust." *Journal of Personality and Social Psychology,* 973, *25,* 419–427.

Schopler, J., and Bateson, N. "A dependence interpretation of the effects of a severe initiation." *Journal of Personality,* 1962, *30,* 633–649.

Senn, D. "Attraction as a Function of Similarity-Dissimilarity in task performance." *Journal of Personality and Social Psychology,* 1971, *18,* 120–123.

Shure, G.; Meeker, R.; and Hansford, E. "The effectiveness of pacifist strategies in bargaining games." *Journal of Conflict Resolution,* 1965, *9,* 106–117.

Solomon, L. "The influence of some types of power relationships and game strategies upon the development of interpersonal trust." *Journal of Abnormal and Social Psychology,* 1960, *61,* 223–230.

Steiner, I. *Group Processes and Productivity.* New York: Academic Press, 1972.

Stoner, J. "A comparison of individual and group decisions, including risk." Unpublished thesis, MIT, 1961.

Sullivan, H. S. *The Interpersonal Theory of Psychiatry.* New York: Norton, 1953.

Triplett, N. "The dynamogenic factors in peace-making and competition." *American Journal of Psychology,* 1898, *4,* 400–408.

Wallach, M.; Kogan, N.; and Bem, D. "Group influence on individual risk taking." *Journal of Abnormal and Social Psychology,* 1962, *65,* 75–86.

Wolfgang, M. (ed.). "Patterns of violence." *Annals of the American Academy of Political and Social Science,* Vol. 364, Philadelphia, 1966, p. 248.

Wolpe, J. *Psychotherapy by Reciprocal Inhibition.* Stanford: Stanford University Press. 1958.

Worchel, P. "Trust and distrust." In W. Austin and S. Worchel (eds.). *The Social Psychology of Intergroup Relations,* Monterey, Calif.: Brooks/Cole, 1979.

Worchel, S., and Cooper, J. *Understanding Social Psychology.* Homewood, Ill.: Dorsey Press, 1976.

Yalom, I. D. *The Theory and Practice of Group Psychotherapy,* 2nd ed. New York: Basic Books, 1975.

Zajonc, R. "Social facilitation." *Science,* 1965, *149,* 269–274.

_____. "Attitudinal effects of mere exposure." *Journal of Personality and Social Psychology,* 1968, *9,* 1–27.

Zand, D. "Trust and managerial problem-solving." *Administrative Science Quarterly,"* 1972, *17,* 229–239.

Zimbardo, P. "The human choice: Individuation, reason, and order versus deindividuation, impulse, and chaos." In W. Arnold and D. Levine (eds.). *Nebraska Symposium on Motivation,* 1969, *17,* 237–307.

# Name Index

# Subject Index